COYOTE CITY
BIG BUCK CITY

COYOTE CITY
BIG BUCK CITY

Two Plays

THE EXILE CLASSICS SERIES, NUMBER TWENTY-NINE

DANIEL DAVID MOSES

With an interview by Nadine Sivak

Publishers of Singular
Fiction, Poetry, Nonfiction, Drama, Translations and Graphic Books

Library and Archives Canada Cataloguing in Publication

Moses, Daniel David, 1952-
[Plays. Selections]
Coyote city ; Big buck city : two plays / Daniel David Moses ;
with an interview by Nadine Sivak.

(The Exile classics series ; number twenty-nine)
Issued in print and electronic formats.
ISBN 978-1-55096-678-7 (softcover).--ISBN 978-1-55096-679-4 (EPUB).--
ISBN 978-1-55096-680-0 (Kindle).--ISBN 978-1-55096-681-7 (PDF)

I. Title. II. Title: Big buck city. III. Series: Exile classics ; no. 29

PS8576.O747A6 2017   C812'.54   C2017-905874-6
                                               C2017-905875-4

Copyright © Daniel David Moses, 2017
Text design and composition, and cover by Michael Callaghan
Typeset in Fairfield font at Moons of Jupiter Studios
Published by Exile Editions / Ontario, Canada ~ www.ExileEditions.com
Printed and bound in Canada by Marquis

We gratefully acknowledge the Canada Council for the Arts,
the Government of Canada, the Ontario Arts Council,
and the Ontario Media Development Corporation
for their support toward our publishing activities.

 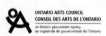 

Canadian sales representation:
The Canadian Manda Group, 664 Annette Street,
Toronto ON M6S 2C8   www.mandagroup.com   416 516 0911

North American and international distribution, and U.S. sales:
Independent Publishers Group, 814 North Franklin Street,
Chicago IL 60610   www.ipgbook.com   toll free: 1 800 888 4741

Coyote City is for Carol
and
Big Buck City is for Eric

Cronies on this expedition

Contents

COYOTE CITY and BIG BUCK CITY:
URBAN WILDERNESS

An interview with Daniel David Moses
by Nadine Sivak

NS: In both plays, the city is characterized as an environment that is openly hostile to Indigenous people. Would your 2017 take on the urban reality be any different?

DDM: When these plays were first written and produced, the presence of Indians, as we were called then, that presence in the city wasn't something that was part of the daily news cycle or the audience's mindset. CBC had even cancelled its one long-running radio magazine, "Our Native Land," focused on aboriginal issues. Maybe I felt the dangers of the city needed to be portrayed with fanciful elements like ghost stories and farcical energies, just to keep the audience from suspending their disbelief. "Indians aren't like that!" I remember my first producer, a fellow Indian, while willing to accept the ghost story in *Coyote City*, just couldn't believe that the middle-class Indians of *Big Buck City* had any reality. Meanwhile, members of my own extended family – nurses, civil servants, teachers, musicians – were definitely middle class. Indians, my producer seemed to feel, should only be as the mainstream imagined them somehow. Now in the aftermath of the TRC and the Idle No More movement and the MMIW commission and, just these last weeks, more reports of aboriginal students dying mysteriously – is it a serial killer? – in the city of Thunder Bay, perhaps the conventions of the thriller or the horror story would be more appropriate. Or very black comedy: I've often thought that the plot of Luis Bunuel's *The Exterminating Angel* might be easily adapted to explore the position of aboriginal people in the contemporary world.

NS: At a number of levels, including character, story and staging, the journey from the beginning of *Coyote City* to the end of *Big Buck City* could be described as one from innocence to experience. Can you comment on this progression and also reflect upon it in terms of your own journey as a playwright?

DDM: Certainly the character of BOO in *Coyote City* and then I guess JACK in *Big Buck City* are thrown into situations with steep learning curves. Both come to see that the world they thought they understood and had a handle on – JACK in particular loses control – is not one that's easy to navigate; BOO because the world clearly has spiritual dimensions like ghosts she'd been too level-headed to consider, and JACK because all his materialistic knowledge of the material world is not the humane way of approaching family relationships. To write these plays I needed to find the right metaphors to connect the spiritual dimensions of the stories to contemporary material realities. For *Coyote City*, it was the image of 'phone calls from the dead' – I found a little documentary paperback that collected such anecdotes. For *Big Buck City*, I needed to be able to see the set, the layout and furnishings of that middle-class living room that JACK and BARBARA had created as their outpost in the human wilderness of the city.

NS: Can you discuss the role of the supernatural and its encroachment on everyday reality in these two plays and in your dramatic works more broadly? What kinds of challenges are inherent in staging the supernatural?

DDM: I think my theatrical ghosts et cetera function as they do in our 'everyday reality' lives, as ways of starting to understand those parts of life that are so complex or so little understood that they don't quite make sense to our limited sensibilities. I've never really experienced a ghost but I know folks have come out of the ghost closet after experiencing the play. And I was once in a room when someone else saw a ghost – he was looking at an angle through a doorway – and, looking back on that moment, I do think I felt the ghost even if I didn't have the psychic tuning to perceive the presence. It really is only in the last century that we've started to understand in an orderly way the ways we sense and make sense of reality, thanks to thinkers like Freud et cetera. His ideas are useful but too new as metaphors to really have imaginative emotional weight that can make works of art both attractive and evocative. The audience recognizes the convention and mostly are willing to go along for the ride. And I figure if Shakespeare can get away with having the occasional spook on his stage, I won't say no to such a strong theatrical metaphor. Why would I want to limit my theatre's possibilities? And if ghosts are too scary, the audience is always welcome to interpret them along Freudian or other psychological lines.

NS: A third play, *Kyotopolis*, picks up on some of the same characters introduced in *Coyote City* and *Big Buck City*. Is the story of the Buck/Fisher family complete? Or might we see some of them again?

DDM: I do have fragments of plays focused around the CLARISSE, BARBARA and RICKY characters still alive somewhere in my imagination. I even started the one about RICKY at one point, a piece called *In the Forest of the City*. I was wondering where he came from and how he got to be who he was. But I'm not sure if I'll ever find my way back to those possibilities. I have just published a short story that takes place in the world and wake of *Kyotopolis*. "The Phantom Heart of Pale Face Andrew" appears in *mitewacimowina: Indigenous Science Fiction and Speculative Storytelling*, edited by Neal McLeod, Theytus Books, 2016.

NS: You have a significant body of work across many forms. What makes a story a play as opposed to another form of fiction? Do your ideas come to you in their ultimate form? Do you ever find yourself feeling hemmed in by the limits of the stage?

DDM: I'm a shy guy who loves the necessary solitude required to do a good job of writing something with weight. I love spending the time with just the words and you do get to experience that with other literary forms like fiction or poetry. But what theatre also offers me in balance is a social experience that's rich and complex. You need to go through the rehearsal process to realize the script's spiritual dimensions or ideas or even just its interesting story. It's great to be the expert for a few days while the director, designers and actors take your knowledge and gradually create the movement, emotion and spectacle of the material theatrical production. It feels to me like an experience in miniature of the best that civilization can offer us as striving and thriving human souls, my version of church, I guess. I usually spend a long time thinking about a story that intrigues me before I find the way to make it a play, a story told with multiple points of view, which again expresses my interest in the social or cultural as opposed to the individual experience. There are uses for one-man shows but it's not my preferred form. Even my poetry is becoming less focused on the single lyrical voice in an effort to be more true to a broader community experience. I kind of like the limits of the stage. They focus the imagination. Freedom of the imagination can just be literary fireworks – the smoke drifts off into the night. A line from I think Dylan Thomas' "Fern Hill" expresses my emotional understanding of the way art gets made: "Time held me green and dying / Though I sang in my chains like the sea."

NS: Both these plays are fairly producible in terms of elements such as cast size and staging requirements. How do considerations around producibility or marketability factor into your playwriting? After over 20 years of writing plays, can you speak in an overarching way about what you hope readers/audience members will come away with?

DDM: It hasn't been my experience starting as a young playwright that plays with six characters are 'fairly producible'. Even as an established voice, it is my plays with fewer characters that have had more success finding the funds to be realized or re-realized. My most ambitious pieces, *Brebeuf's Ghost* and *Kyotopolis*, workshopped with student casts at universities with crowds of characters – the spectacle of a crowd on stage is one I envy – but of course my subject matter, Canadian indigenous experience, probably won't get productions in our country's still colonial mindset. My current project I'm imagining for two actors and though producibility or marketability may be in the back of my mind, I'm fairly certain the size of this cast is because of how I perceive the play's subject matter and the proper dichotomous way to try to explore and express it. I hope the audience will be willing to also view it as an adventure.

Nadine Sivak is a graduate of the University of Toronto's Centre for Drama, Theatre and Performance Studies where her doctoral thesis, which explored post-colonial representations of identity, included a chapter on the work of Daniel David Moses. She has been an instructor of drama at Brock University and currently works for the Department of Canadian Heritage in Toronto.

COYOTE CITY

The ghost said to Coyote, "Here we have conditions different from those you have in the land of the living. When it gets dark here it has dawned in your land and when it dawns for us, it is growing dark for you." (Coyote and the Shadow People)

To be seen is the ambition of ghosts and to be remembered the ambition of the dead. (Norman O. Brown)

COYOTE CITY was produced by Native Earth Performing Arts Inc. at the Native Canadian Centre of Toronto from 17 May to 5 June 1988, with the following cast:

JOHNNY	Gordon Odjig
LENA	Alanis King
BOO	Tina Louise Bomberry
MARTHA	Margaret Cozry
THOMAS	Ron Cook
CLARISSE	Gloria Eshkibok

Directed by Anne Anglin

CHARACTERS

JOHNNY, a young Indian man, a ghost.

LENA, a young Indian woman.

BOO, a young Indian woman, LENA's younger sister.

MARTHA, a middle-aged Indian woman, LENA's mother.

THOMAS, a middle-aged Indian man, a minister.

CLARISSE, an Indian woman, a hooker.

SETTING

The play is set in a darkness complicated only by spotlights and the shadows of the characters and the few necessary properties. It happens just yesterday on a reserve and then in the city.

ACT ONE

ACT ONE, SCENE ONE

Darkness.

JOHNNY: Give me a drink. I need a drink. Shit. I'm over here you bugger. *(a spot reveals him, he speaks to it)* I'm almost empty here. Come on and dispense with the booze.

Please, man, I'm good for it. You can trust me. I'll pay you tomorrow first thing. Come on. Come on, man, really.

Hey, you want my knife? It's a real beaut. Look at all the things, man, the gadgets. Hey, you can even cut your toenails. Come on, guy, just one more beer. Shit.

Hey, how about a date with a real doll? Shit, man, she's fresh from the bush. I'll give you her number. Real pretty Indian chick. What do you say? What do you say?

How about a story my granddad gave me? A real good story, man. A love story. Come on, man, the ladies really love to hear this story. Shit, it gets them all loose. You like loose ladies, don't you? Just another beer, man. Just one. That's all.

(to the darkness) Acting like I'm not here, like he can't see me. Acting like I'm just another drunk Indian. Think he thinks I've had enough? Do you think that too? Do you think I've had enough? Enough? Shit.

4

You think I've had too much. Well, who the fuck are you anyway? I don't know you. I don't know you. Shit, you're not even real. I know I need a drink when I meet you. I look at you and I need a drink. Hey, you're nothing but a bunch of spooks. That's why I got the shakes. You're the ones took Coyote in when he was looking for his woman. But no way you're tricking me. No way. I'm too smart for you. You can't get away with all that stuper-shitting with me. You're not going to get away with anything with me. You're going to buy me a drink. Shit, yeah, you're going to buy me a fucking drink.

ACT ONE, SCENE TWO

A telephone rings a party line ring. A spot reveals it. LENA enters and answers it just after the fourth ring.

LENA: Hello. Hello. Someone there?

JOHNNY'S
VOICE: *(a poor connection)* Lena. Lena, is that you?

LENA: Who's this?

JOHNNY'S
VOICE: Oh Lena, babe, don't you recognize me?

LENA: Johnny?

JOHNNY'S
VOICE: Lena, don't hang up, please.

LENA: Johnny. I'm not.

JOHNNY'S
VOICE: Shit, please, I got to talk to you.

LENA: I'm listening, Johnny. I'm not hanging up now.

JOHNNY'S
VOICE: I'm not drunk, babe. You know me.

LENA: I shouldn't have yelled before. You sound like long distance.

JOHNNY'S
VOICE: Shit, Lena, you know what it's like, this place? Nobody will talk to me. They look right through you, like you're invisible.

LENA: That's crazy talk, Johnny.

JOHNNY'S
VOICE: No. No, there's nobody I can talk to. They won't even give me a beer. Babe, you should come.

LENA: Didn't we say we'd wait? We don't have the money.

JOHNNY'S
VOICE: Oh babe, I'm fucking lonely. I miss you. Shit I think about the way you looked. That time down by the river. Do you remember? The way you looked down at me. I loved you making them little moaning sounds.

LENA: Stop it, Johnny.

JOHNNY'S
VOICE: Your sweat was so sweet, babe. Better than wine. Makes me thirsty just talking about it. Oh babe, the way we did it together. We'd be like that again, babe, like last summer. Didn't we have fun? Oh baby, you'd be my booze.

LENA: Oh Johnny, you're so crazy.

JOHNNY'S
VOICE: Shit, Lena, don't you know I love you?

LENA: Where are you? Where are you, Johnny? I'll come. I want to be with you. Tell me where you are.

JOHNNY'S VOICE:	I'm in the Dollar, the shitty Silver Dollar.
LENA:	I'll come to the city, Johnny. I'll meet you there. I'll be there soon as I can tomorrow.
JOHNNY'S VOICE:	Oh babe, I can't wait.
LENA:	No more waiting, Johnny. I'm on my way.
JOHNNY'S VOICE:	Oh babe, are you really?
LENA:	Sure thing, Johnny, sure thing.
JOHNNY'S VOICE:	I love you, Lena. Shit I love you.

ACT ONE, SCENE THREE

A dial tone. A spot reveals LENA still holding the phone. BOO enters.

BOO: Hey, who was on the phone?

LENA: You almost gave me a heart attack, Boo.

BOO: So what else is new?

LENA: Don't be so loud.

BOO: Loud?

LENA: Loud. You'll wake up Momma.

BOO: I'm not the one chattering her head off on the party line at three a.m.

LENA: Hush up, will you. Go back to bed.

BOO: If she's awake it's not because of me.

LENA: Let's both of us be quiet.

BOO: If she's awake, it's from worrying over you.

LENA: Can't you keep it down?

BOO: She hasn't had a solid night's sleep since you started acting up.

LENA: Leave me alone.

BOO: You're such a phony, Lena. You don't give a shit about Ma.

LENA: I'm going back to bed.

BOO: Haven't you spent enough time there?

LENA: Let me by, Boo.

BOO: You can't go on acting like this.

LENA: I'm not acting.

BOO: Six months, Lena.

LENA: Let me through, Little Sister.

BOO: I'm tired of washing your pillow of dark and secret heartache. Tears and snot, tears and snot.

LENA: That's over now. Over. I promise.

BOO: A likely story. When did you ever do your share?

LENA: You won't have to do my share no more. It's a sure thing.

BOO: Lena, if you just talk about it, it won't hurt so bad.

LENA: You think you're smart.

BOO: Think of Ma. If she sees you in the middle of your famous I Walk Like A Zombie act again—

LENA: You think you know it all, don't you?

BOO: No I don't, Lena. I don't know who was on the phone.

LENA: Shut up, Boo. Shut the fuck up!

BOO: Shut the fuck up? Now who's being loud?

LENA: Out of my way. You're a brat. Nothing but a spoiled brat.

BOO: You woke her up and you're leaving me to suffer for it?

LENA: I can still make you cry.

BOO: Did I miss it? Did you shed some light on the mystery caller?

LENA: You're asking for it.

BOO: Yup. Who was on the phone?

Enter MARTHA.

MARTHA: Stop that, Boo. Stop that now.

LENA: Let go of me. You're hurting me.

MARTHA: Leave your sister alone. I can't believe it. Let go of her. Let go. Now both of you come over here. Come on. What you girls doing out of bed at this hour? Boo?

BOO: I'm sorry, Ma. Lena was—

LENA: Don't lie, Little Sister.

MARTHA: You're supposed to be grownups.

BOO: I suppose you were just asking the night operator about
            her operation for half an hour.

MARTHA: Night operator?

BOO: She was on the phone.

MARTHA: It did ring then. What's wrong, Lena? Who called?

LENA: There's nothing wrong, Momma.

MARTHA: But someone did call?

BOO: Lena, she asked you a question.

LENA: Leave me alone.

BOO: This is getting boring.

MARTHA: Be quiet, Boo. Is something wrong, Lena? Answer me.

LENA: Not in front of her.

BOO: Okay. *(she turns her back)* How's this?

MARTHA: Boo, that's enough—

BOO: Is that you, Ma?

MARTHA: Daughter.

BOO: Yeah, Ma?

MARTHA: You've had your fun. Now go make a pot of tea.

BOO: I don't drink that stuff, Ma. Gives you a shaky head.

MARTHA: You're making it for me, Daughter.

BOO: Oh. Okay, Ma.

MARTHA: Thank you, Boo.

BOO: Should I maybe like make you your toast too?

MARTHA: That would be nice.

BOO: Because look. There's already light out in the east, so it's almost time for breakfast.

MARTHA: Thank you, Boo.

BOO: And all those birdies out there, chattering their little heads off, I mean, we'll probably never get back to sleep now—

MARTHA: That's enough, Boo.

BOO: How about some honey, Ma?

MARTHA: I'm on a diet, Daughter!

BOO: Okay. Okay, I'm going. But she'll tell me later anyway, Lena. *(she exits)*

MARTHA: Oh Lena, sometimes your little sis is almost too much for me.

LENA: I'm sorry we woke you, Momma.

MARTHA: Why do I still have to pull you apart at my age?

LENA: I told her not to be loud. I told her you'd wake up.

MARTHA: Oh you can't tell your sister a thing. You know that. But she just wants to help.

LENA: I just wish she'd mind her own business.

MARTHA: Your sister's just worried for you, Lena. Both of us are. We don't want you upset again. You need your rest. That wasn't bad new, was it, on the phone?

LENA: No, Momma, she's not worried. She doesn't care about me.

MARTHA: Now Lena, that's not true. Boo's your sister.

LENA: She's jealous. Just jealous. And it's too bad, because he never really liked her.

MARTHA: Who? Who you talking about?

LENA: It's so dumb and sort of sad. But that's why she's after me. She can't get over it. She can't admit it, that Johnny loves me.

MARTHA: Johnny?

LENA: I should tell her the truth. I should tell her, shouldn't I? To settle it. She's got to grow up someday.

MARTHA: What do you mean, Lena?

LENA: That it was Johnny that called. And that he called me, all the way from the city.

MARTHA: Lena, that can't be.

LENA: I don't like to hurt her, Momma. I know how she must feel. I know how I'd be if he didn't love me no more.

MARTHA: Lena, Lena, look at me.

LENA: But he shouldn't be between us. I'll tell her.

MARTHA: Lena, stop. Don't tell your sister that.

LENA: Don't worry, Momma. Boo can take it. She's strong.

MARTHA: No, Lena, no. You've got to listen to me.

LENA: Boo! Boo come in here!

MARTHA: Oh Daughter, you're not awake, you're not awake, you're dreaming.

LENA: Stop listening at the keyhole, Little Sister.

BOO enters.

BOO: The word is eavesdropping. And I wasn't. With all those birds twittering away, it wouldn't have done no good.

LENA: You still want to know about the phone?

BOO: Is her memory going again?

MARTHA: This is no time for jokes.

BOO: What is it, Ma?

LENA: Know who called me? All the way from the city?

BOO: The city? Was it Aunty?

MARTHA: You had a bad dream, Lena, a bad dream.

LENA: You know who it was?

BOO: I was doing better listening to the birds.

LENA: I'm going to tell you. But you got to listen close. I want
            it to get through your head. I don't want this between
            us no more.

BOO: Okay. Enlighten me. This must be serious stuff.

MARTHA: It's starting all over again, Boo.

LENA: It was Johnny. Yeah, Johnny.

BOO: Wait a minute, Lena—

LENA: No, you wait, Little Sister. You wait and get it through
            your head. Johnny called me. He didn't ask for you.
            He didn't even mention you. He called me. Under-
            stand?

BOO: You're serious, aren't you?

LENA: I'm sorry, Little Sister. That's the way it is.

MARTHA: Oh my baby, you were doing so good.

LENA: What's the matter, Momma?

BOO: What's the matter! She's gone cuckoo. She's gone real cuckoo this time. You're out of your nest, you know that?

LENA: Don't be mad, Boo. Why can't you just admit he loves me?

BOO: It's kind of beside the point.

MARTHA: Daughter, listen to your sister.

LENA: Momma, tell her he loves me. I'm sorry, Boo, really.

MARTHA: Lena, try to remember about Johnny.

LENA: I'm going to see him tonight, Momma.

BOO: Lena, you know Johnny is dead.

LENA: We're meeting at the Silver Dollar.

BOO: Lena, Johnny is dead. He's dead.

LENA: Little Sister, you mustn't cry. Everything's going to be okay.

BOO: I'm not crying.

MARTHA: Lena, listen to Boo. She's telling you the truth.

LENA: Oh Momma, she's got a broken heart.

MARTHA: No, Lena, remember. Johnny's gone.

LENA: He's waiting for me.

BOO: Lena, there was a fight, a knife. Remember that goofy knife of his? The Silver Dollar's the place he got killed.

LENA: Do you think he had a good time? Visiting his folks out west. I can't wait to hear about it.

MARTHA: Lena, remember, the police called.

BOO: They even showed up here. Remember how that cop car almost got stuck in the lane?

MARTHA: They asked about where he was from.

LENA: Momma, why didn't you ask me?

MARTHA: Lena, it was in the newspaper. Remember the newspaper?

LENA: Don't believe everything you read, Momma. It's crazy. The newspapers lie. Isn't that what you always say, Boo? A likely story? They're always telling lies about us. Isn't that true?

BOO: But why lie about a guy like Johnny?

LENA: You know why, Boo. Johnny was never one of them Indians they write about. Johnny's special.

BOO: Johnny was just a regular guy.

LENA:	The day you brought him home you said he was bright.
MARTHA:	Lena, listen. He was just a drunk.
LENA:	Momma, he's going to do something real special someday.
MARTHA:	Lena. Lena, where are you going?
LENA:	Got to pack, Momma. I'm going to be with him that day. *(she exits)*
MARTHA:	Lena. Oh my poor baby.
BOO:	What a joke. He was such a jerk.
MARTHA:	What are we going to do?
BOO:	Always calling up drunk. That's why long distance gives me the creeps.
MARTHA:	Turn on a light. I can't think.
BOO:	Ringing in the middle of the night, waking us up.
MARTHA:	I thought this was all over with, Boo.
BOO:	Ma, seems like there are telephones on the other side.
MARTHA:	Don't talk nonsense.
BOO:	Calls like this don't come from a person, Ma.

MARTHA: Boo, how do we get through to her?

BOO: Christ, I don't know. Call her on the telephone?

MARTHA: Don't be smart.

BOO: Disembodied. That's the word.

MARTHA dials a local number.

BOO: We could all be spooks as far as telephones are con-
            cerned.

The telephone rings a different party line ring.

BOO: Ma, who you calling?

MARTHA: I hope he's there. It is early yet. He won't be making
            calls.

BOO: Ma, talk about spooks, you're not calling him. (*she
            stops the call*)

MARTHA: Who else can help us?

BOO: Ma, we don't need him.

MARTHA: `You're ungrateful, Boo. He helped me a lot. Those
            first few weeks were so bad.

BOO: Well, we don't need him now.

MARTHA: Didn't you hear what your sister said?

BOO: Ma, we'll help her, but just us, just family.

MARTHA: This is worse than before. And Thomas was your father's best friend. He is family.

BOO: With family like him, who needs vultures? He's only around when there's trouble.

MARTHA: Trouble is his business.

BOO: Is that on his calling card?

MARTHA: He's a man of the cloth. Don't you laugh. He's a man of the cloth and there's trouble now and I don't know what to do. And you don't either.

BOO: Ma, we could just talk to her.

MARTHA: Talk? I'm tired of talk. That's all I been doing. Six months of talk. Talk talk talk. I don't know what else to talk about. What else can I say? 'The hurt will go away, the hurt will go away'? It doesn't get through to her. I'm tired of it. I'm tired. I've said all I can say. (*she dials again and the different ring recommences*)

BOO: Ma, let me. I'll do it. I'll talk to her.

MARTHA: Oh you, you leave her alone.

A spot reveals THOMAS picking up his receiver, the ringing stops.

BOO: No, Ma, listen to me. Let me try.

MARTHA: Be quiet! Hello. Hello, Thomas? Are you there?

THOMAS: Is that Martha?

MARTHA: I'm sorry. It's awful early—

BOO: Hang up, Ma. Hang up. We can handle this our-
            selves.

MARTHA: Be quiet when I tell you. You're supposed to be a
            grownup. Thomas?

THOMAS: I'm here, Martha.

MARTHA: Thomas, I...

THOMAS: Yes, Martha?

MARTHA: It's Lena.

BOO exits.

THOMAS: What is it? What has she done? Are you all right?

MARTHA: Please. I can't talk about it on the phone.

THOMAS: Did she injure herself?

MARTHA: Thomas, not on the phone.

THOMAS: All right, Martha. As you wish. Pray to our Lord for
            strength, Martha. I'll be right over.

MARTHA: Thank you. Thank you, Thomas. I'll do as you say.
            Hurry. (*she hangs up, her spot fades out*)

THOMAS: Praise the Lord, Martha. Praise our Saviour as I do. I
            offer thanks to Him again this morning for bringing
            you back into my life. I thank Him for bringing me

into this new day, for allowing me to be of service to such a fine lady and her beautiful, beautiful daughters.

Heavenly Father, in the name of your son Jesus, I again give myself like a present to you. I pray and ask Jesus to be Lord of my life. In my heart I believe and so I say with my mouth: He has been raised from the dead. Jesus has been raised from the dead. He is the light of my life. Jesus enters my heart. I am saved, yea, I am saved, reborn a Christian child, a babe of Almighty God. Oh my heart has been raised up again like the sun this day from the dead.

ACT ONE, SCENE FOUR

A spot reveals LENA packing. BOO enters.

BOO: Lena. Lena, I got something to say.

LENA: What is it now?

BOO: Do you know what you're doing?

LENA: Little Sister, I can pack my own suitcase.

BOO: That's not what I'm talking about.

LENA: I should have kept quiet.

BOO: Lena, this isn't very bright.

LENA: He never loved you, Boo. Never.

BOO: Lena, stop it. I don't care about Johnny.

LENA: That's good, I suppose, if it's true. But it must be hard. You always been so jealous of me.

BOO: Lena, I'm not jealous.

LENA: You can't help being born first. You'll understand when you grow up.

BOO: There's nothing to be jealous of. Boy, is there nothing.

LENA: Oh Little Sister, is that how you feel?

BOO: Lena, I care about you.

LENA:	I hope it's true. I don't want to leave you mad at me.
BOO:	Oh Lena, I'm not mad.
LENA:	Then you don't mind about this?
BOO:	Hey, that sweater's mine.
LENA:	I want to borrow it. In case it's cold.
BOO:	Aunty sent it to me.
LENA:	If you don't want me to take it, just say so.
BOO:	So. So-so-so. You got sweaters of your own.
LENA:	Maybe it won't be cold.
BOO:	Lena, I'm sorry. Come on. Sit down a moment and talk to me.
LENA:	I don't need the sweater.
BOO:	Come on. Take it. And talk to me. If you're going away I won't see you for a long time. I'm going to miss my Big Sister.
LENA:	I don't need it, Boo, thanks anyway.
BOO:	Tell me about Johnny. What you going to do if he's not there?
LENA:	Oh Boo, don't hurt yourself.
BOO:	I'm not hurting myself, Lena.

LENA: You believe that, don't you? How did you get so
            tough? You must be disappointed.

BOO: Disappointed? Well, okay, disappointed. Well, why
            shouldn't I be disappointed? He was my friend and
            off you go and screw around with him.

LENA: Little Sister, we couldn't help it. It happens.

BOO: As if you would know. If you hadn't been boozing it up
            all the time—

LENA: He wasn't boozing it up. Not when he was with me.
            He didn't need to booze it up when he was with me.

BOO: Now wait a minute, Lena—

LENA: You think we didn't talk about you, about us? We did.
            I felt funny about it, going out with him, 'til he told
            me how you teased him.

BOO: What is it? What did he say?

LENA: Coming on bright-eyed and smiling. Then only letting
            him hold your hand.

BOO: I wasn't ready to get serious. He knew that.

LENA: You weren't ready? You're nothing but a tease. A cock
            tease. That's what he said. Walking out with him like
            you cared.

BOO: Walking is safer than parking. And I did like him. I
            did. He knew a lot of interesting stuff.

LENA:	Interesting stuff! He was interested in you.
BOO:	Stuff about the old folks out west. You know, old stories.
LENA:	I know. He told me how you bugged him, asking him about those stupid stories.
BOO:	Look, Lena, he didn't mind telling me. I mean some of them stories are real comical. He liked telling them.
LENA:	Why can't you learn the lesson, Little Sister? You can't treat a man like a book.
BOO:	There's more to life than fucking around.
LENA:	As if you would know. Boo, if you don't use it, you lose it.
BOO:	That's Johnny talking, isn't it?
LENA:	That's the interesting stuff he knew. Not your fairytale bullshit.
BOO:	Lena, there's this one he told me. It's like right now almost.
LENA:	Oh Little Sister, you'll end up an old maid.
BOO:	It's a Coyote story. About when his wife died? Well, Coyote tried to bring her back from the land of the dead.
LENA:	Boo, this is real life. And Johnny's a real man. A flesh and blood man. You should try flesh and blood.

BOO:	Johnny really liked this story. I think it was his favourite.
LENA:	I never heard of it. We don't need your stupid stories. They got nothing to do with us. We're not living in the bush no more.
BOO:	Lena, wait. You got to listen.
LENA:	Get off the suitcase, Boo.
BOO:	I'm trying to help you.
LENA:	Then get off. Get off! *(she pushes BOO off)* Now I know why Momma calls you her cross. I can't find my gold chain. Yeah, the one Johnny gave me. Did you hide it again? Did you?
BOO:	No.
LENA:	I'll find it anyway. You can't outsmart me, you brat. *(she exits)*
BOO:	*(speaking to the light)* Oh Lena. I tell you, Coyote and his wife were living together once. And they were happy, happy 'til his wife got sick, so very sick she died. And Coyote got lonesome, so lonesome he didn't do a thing but cry. Oh he cried for his wife. And Lena, you know, Johnny said that a spirit came from the land of the dead to Coyote and asked him, Coyote, say, do you miss that woman? I can take you where she is, but you got to do just exactly as I say. So of course Coyote said, Yeah, sure, I'll do exactly as you say. Only take me where my woman is.

ACT ONE, SCENE FIVE

A spot comes up. MARTHA and THOMAS enter.

MARTHA: Thank you for coming so quick.

THOMAS: You only have to beckon.

MARTHA: Thank you, Thomas. Come on. Sit down.

THOMAS: I came overland, the short cut down along the river.

MARTHA: Thank you, Thomas. I—

THOMAS: Our people surviving here in the wilderness all these years. I don't understand it. Unless He watched over us then too like He did the Israelites. Even though we were savages, ignorant—

MARTHA: Well, I pray He's watching over us now, Thomas.

THOMAS: I beg your pardon, Martha. You have something to tell.

MARTHA: Thomas, it's Lena.

THOMAS: Martha, blessed are they that mourn, for they shall be comforted. Be patient with your daughter and you too shall be comforted.

MARTHA: But Thomas, she's leaving.

THOMAS: Leaving? How surprising glad tidings can be. So this is how quickly our prayers can be answered. Her wound has been healed. Oh we must praise the Lord.

MARTHA: But Thomas, she thinks that boy's alive. She wants to go meet him.

THOMAS: What boy, Martha?

MARTHA: Johnny. Lena thinks Johnny's alive. He called her last night, she says. She's in her room right now, packing to go meet him.

THOMAS: He called her?

MARTHA: On the telephone. Thomas, what can I do? I tried talking to her, you know how I tried. Boo's trying to get through to her now too. She was doing so good lately.

THOMAS: My dear, this is so cunning. A ghost on the line. You know we must pray against it. You have been praying, haven't you?

MARTHA: Yes, of course I have, Thomas. But she wants to go off to the city.

THOMAS: The city. No, she must not go there. The city's full of emptiness. It's got to be the Dark One tempting her. We must not allow that to happen. Martha, we must restrain her somehow.

MARTHA: Restrain her? You mean like ropes? But that's awful. I couldn't do that.

THOMAS: Martha, please, it's for her own good. The wound in her spirit has been infected. We must let the Lord clean it out. We must have patience. Are not His ways beyond our understanding?

MARTHA: I don't know. It's so wrong. Oh, Thomas, I'm afraid.

THOMAS: There's nothing to fear, Martha, dear. I will be with you. And the Lord our light is upon us.

MARTHA: Promise not to laugh at me, Thomas.

THOMAS: Martha, have I ever mocked you?

MARTHA: Thomas, what if Johnny's still there?

THOMAS: Martha, the boy was killed.

MARTHA: That's right, Thomas. I know.

THOMAS: A boy like that always ends up in question. I could see it in him. He had lost his way. Him bleeding his life onto the floor of a bar.

MARTHA: I was scared when I heard about the blood, Thomas.

THOMAS: I have seen that sort of thing before. Why do our boys waste themselves this way, Martha? Can't they see that Jesus already shed His own precious blood for all our sakes?

MARTHA: I never liked him. What he made Lena do.

THOMAS: She came home to you. She came back to you.

MARTHA: I didn't know her. I didn't know a daughter of mine could act like that kind of woman. I never taught her that. I taught her to be good.

THOMAS: That boy was just wild, Martha. Not really bad. Just lost.

MARTHA: Thomas, I felt happy when he got killed.

THOMAS: Martha, I think we must ask for forgiveness for—

MARTHA: I thought about it, that knife in him, and I was happy. He was bad. When Boo read it out of the paper to me about his body going west, I thought, Now that's good. That ends it.

THOMAS: The Lord forgive you.

MARTHA: But then Lena got so sick then. I supposed that's what I deserved.

THOMAS: Some of our wounds are too full of pain. They flood our hearts.

MARTHA: Thomas, I'm afraid, afraid of his spirit. His spirit. Him and Lena were so in love, he might really be there, in that Silver Dollar place.

THOMAS: Martha, how can you say that? It's almost sacrilege.

MARTHA: Are not His ways mysterious?

THOMAS: Yes, that is so. I think we must pray to the Lord now for guidance.

MARTHA: Thomas, when Lenard died, after he died, he came back once.

THOMAS: Who came back?

MARTHA:	Lenard. In the middle of the night. At the foot of my bed he stood. I tried to touch him again, Thomas, but he just turned away. Just turned away. I wanted to follow him.
THOMAS:	You loved him that much.
MARTHA:	Thomas, I would have killed myself to go with him.
THOMAS:	Martha, life is a gift. It is not a thing we dare throw away.
MARTHA:	Why did he turn away, Thomas?
THOMAS:	Why? I don't know. Perhaps the Lord was trying your faith.
MARTHA:	Thomas, Lena's going to the city to die.
THOMAS:	No, Martha, no, that cannot be true.
MARTHA:	It is, Thomas, it is. She wants to follow that boy.
THOMAS:	Our God is not a vengeful God, Martha. She won't die. She won't be allowed to die. The Lord, the Lord and I will be with her. Yes. This is our test, our punishment. I'll go with her. We will meet the devil in his darkness. Our faith is our lantern. Nothing can happen to us.
MARTHA:	Thomas, are you sure?
THOMAS:	It's so clear, Martha. This is our trial, but by the Lord's grace, we will rise again and return victorious from

that dark place. I'll show her the way, the truth, and bring her back to the light of her family.

MARTHA: I can't let her go.

THOMAS: Martha, don't you believe in the Lord? He will forgive us all our faults if we pass this test. He will forgive you what you thought about that boy. Don't you believe me? Don't you believe in me?

MARTHA: I do, Thomas. I do.

THOMAS: We must face up to this evil Johnny-thing.

MARTHA: I guess you're right.

THOMAS: You must pray for us, Martha. Pray for us. Will you pray with me now?

MARTHA: All right.

THOMAS: Heavenly Father, in the name of your son Jesus, lighten our darkness and by thy mercy, defend us from all the great perils of the city. Let us emerge victorious, resurrected from—

LENA enters with suitcase, BOO in pursuit.

BOO: Hold it right there. You're not getting out of my sight.

LENA: Momma, make her leave me alone.

MARTHA: I'm sorry about this.

THOMAS: Don't concern yourself, dear lady.

LENA: Will you get off my back?

BOO: This looks more like an arm to me.

THOMAS: Barbara. Barbara, please. Let your dear sister go. Don't disturb her any further.

BOO: Disturb her any further? Is that possible?

MARTHA: Daughter, mind your manners.

LENA: Momma, how far did you drive yesterday?

BOO: Sorry, Rev, we're having us a family problem here.

MARTHA: Just to the store.

THOMAS: I know all about it, my dear. Believe in me. Trust me.

LENA: Do you think there's gas left?

BOO: What are you talking about?

MARTHA: There's plenty of gas.

BOO: What's he talking about, Ma?

MARTHA: We have a plan, Boo.

THOMAS: Lena, dear, your mother and I have been talking. So you're off on a journey today?

LENA: Yes, I'm going to meet Johnny. He's back from his trip.

THOMAS: How wonderful for you. I was wondering. Might I
            accompany you? I too need to go into the city.

BOO: What's going on here?

LENA: I'm going right away. I got to be there tonight.

THOMAS: Excellent, my dear, most excellent. I need to tend to
            an emergency there. Isn't that so, Martha?

BOO: Reverend, do you realize this woman is not exactly
            clear-headed?

MARTHA: Boo, let the Reverend be. He knows what he's doing.

THOMAS: I can do a share of the driving, child.

LENA: It is a long way. And you can bring the car back too.
            That makes sense, doesn't it, Momma?

MARTHA: That sounds good to me, Daughter.

BOO: Ma, what are you talking about? Lena, give me those
            keys. You can't—

THOMAS: Damn it, Barbara! Listen. Let your sister go. Trust
            me.

BOO: You get your hand off me. What the hell's going on?
            Have you all gone crazy?

MARTHA: Let your sister be. She and the Reverend have a long
            way to go today.

LENA: I'll go warm up the car. (*she exits*)

BOO: Lena! Ma, why you doing this?

MARTHA: The Reverend understands what this is all about.

THOMAS: I'm sorry, dear child. I know you have little faith in me
                but your mother and I think this will bring—

BOO: Listen, Father, I've got as much faith in you as I do in
                Santa Claus.

THOMAS: You don't have to have faith in me. Put your faith in
                the Lord.

BOO: Jesus saves?

THOMAS: Jesus does save. And I am His servant. And I am your
                mother's friend and your sister's guide. I will bring her
                face to face with the darkness of the city and back
                safely again. I will—

A car horn impatiently.

THOMAS: Goodbye, Martha, lest she leave me behind. Barbara.
                Praise the Lord.

MARTHA: Praise Him. We'll pray for you. We will.

THOMAS exits.

MARTHA: Stay where you are, Daughter. Let them go. Stay put.
                Stay.

BOO: I'm your daughter, not your dog. Shit, Ma, this is no
                way to help Lena.

MARTHA: Watch your tongue. Lena will be all right. The Rever-
            end understands what's going on. He's a good friend
            to us.

BOO: Ma, she doesn't need that sort of good friend. She's
            not that lonesome. I mean she's gone out of her tree.
            She needs a head doctor.

MARTHA: I'm not so sure.

BOO: Ma, we were doing better just talking to her. We were.
            We were getting through. We should have sat on her
            if we had to.

MARTHA: It wasn't doing no good.

BOO: It was, Ma, it was.

MARTHA: You call getting a call like that getting better? There
            are some things even you don't understand.

BOO: What's that supposed to mean?

MARTHA: You think you're smart because you been to school.
            Well, you don't know everything. This is a spiritual
            problem.

BOO: Ma, spirits have got nothing to do with this.

MARTHA: The Reverend says we must pray. He says this is the
            Lord's way of testing us. Don't you laugh. He's put his
            problem behind him.

BOO: Problem? What problem?

MARTHA: I don't know if he'd like you knowing about it.

BOO: Ma, the guy already gives me the willies. He shakes your hand like he wants to get his all over you.

MARTHA: He just tries too hard.

BOO: So what's the problem? Tell me, Ma.

MARTHA: He had a problem with drink. When he was in the city.

BOO: Our Rev's an old alky?

MARTHA: He wound up in hospital. You don't know how sad he looked.

BOO: I can imagine.

MARTHA: Do you know, Boo, every time he coughed, he coughed up blood?

BOO: I said I can imagine. A reborn alcoholic and a zombie princess. Shit, Ma, I'm going after them.

MARTHA: Boo, wait. They took the car.

BOO: I'll borrow one. Clare or Bee would let me.

MARTHA: No, they're gone to work by now. And anyway I can't explain this to them. I won't.

BOO: I won't tell them a thing.

MARTHA: No. It'll take too long. If we walk over to the Indian Line, we can catch a bus.

BOO: You're coming with me?

MARTHA: Of course. Call the station. Find out when the next one comes along.

BOO: The bus takes too long. If we had a car—

MARTHA: I won't have the whole reserve know Lena sees ghosts. I won't. She's no pagan. It's bad enough as it is. What are you looking at?

BOO: We'll lose them, Ma.

MARTHA: We know where they'll be tonight. She should be all right 'til then.

BOO: But Ma, who knows what will happen if they get to the city?

MARTHA: Go on. Call the station. I'll make a lunch. *(she exits)*

BOO: *(she dials the station and waits)* Hello? Okay, okay, but hurry. Please hurry.

            Hurry. We got to get there before dark.

Spots in a row come up, suggesting street lights.

BOO: Once it got dark, Coyote could see them, the dead people. They were just getting up, having their breakfasts. It's like they're awake when we're dreaming, living new lives while we're dead to the world. They had

40

their own horses and food and clothes and everything, but everything, themselves included, was made
out of darkness, out of different bits of shadow.
Coyote soon recognized many people he used to
know, so many of his old pals around the fire there,
he almost forgot about looking for his wife in that
lodge big as night. *(her spot goes out)*

*Enter CLARISSE, strolling the street, checking out the action. She
smiles and waves at an approaching car, then, as it passes her by, gives it
the finger. She laughs at herself and continues. She stops under a light
and checks the street before getting a joint out of her purse. She stops
before she strikes her match when she hears:*

THOMAS: *(off)* Wait, child. Wait! Don't go so fast.

LENA enters, THOMAS in pursuit. CLARISSE drops her match.

LENA: Come on. We're going to be late.

THOMAS: We have to take care. It's getting dark. This is a place
             of great peril.

LENA: We've lost too much time already.

THOMAS: Please, child, I'm sorry. I'm not used to walking on
             concrete.

LENA: He must be thinking I forgot.

THOMAS: I'm sure I got blisters on my feet. It's such a long jour-
             ney for a single day. If only we had taken refreshment
             along the road.

LENA: Hey. Hey, mister. Do you know the way—?

THOMAS: You can't approach white people like that. We could get in trouble. They'll summon the police. They don't want to see Indians. Lena, they don't like us. They'll put us down into the gutter. They'll keep us in the darkness there.

LENA: You're talking crazy. Excuse me, please.

CLARISSE: Hiya, kid. What can I do you for?

LENA: We're a little lost.

CLARISSE: Hey, isn't everybody? What's going on anyway? You look worse for wear.

LENA: Well, he crashed our car.

THOMAS: That's not exactly the manner it occurred.

LENA: How do I get to the Silver Dollar?

CLARISSE: The Buck?

LENA: You know where that place is?

CLARISSE: What you taking this kid to the Buck for, old man?

THOMAS: I'm not doing that.

CLARISSE: You should pick up something your own age.

THOMAS: I'm not taking her there. I want her to come home with me.

CLARISSE: You ought to be ashamed. Has he tried anything, kid?

LENA: No, it's not like that. He's supposed to be helping me. There's a friend of mine I'm supposed to be meeting.

CLARISSE: A friend, eh? The way you say it, is your special guy?

LENA: Sort of. He says he's my finance. Fiancé.

CLARISSE: A card, is he? And you met him at the Buck. Fuck. Some people have all the luck.

THOMAS: I must ask you to excuse us.

CLARISSE: No, it's no problem at all, Tommy.

THOMAS: How did you know my name?

CLARISSE: I've met the likes of you before.

THOMAS: I beg your pardon?

CLARISSE: You been here before. I see the city in your eyes. So you just watch it.

THOMAS: I don't understand you.

CLARISSE: Never mind, Tommy. Tom, Dick or Harry, it don't matter. Say, your friend's not named, say, Richard or Harold?

LENA: Johnny.

CLARISSE: That's his real name? Christ, that's silly.

THOMAS: Don't you use His name in vain.

CLARISSE: We're not going to take Johnny's name in vain, now are we?

THOMAS: Lena, come along, let's not bother this lady. I can see she has other things to concern her.

CLARISSE: Lena. That's nice. I'm Clarisse. Want me to help you find your sweetie?

LENA: Really? Hey, she'll show us the way.

CLARISSE: I'm offering my expert advice.

LENA: Thank you. Isn't this great?

THOMAS: We really don't want to trouble you.

CLARISSE: No problem, chum. This could be fun.

THOMAS: We mustn't be a bother.

CLARISSE: I was heading over there later anyway. I'm in the mood for slumming. Even more than usual.

LENA: Reverend, if you don't want to come, it's okay. You have enough money for a bus?

THOMAS: Lena, you mustn't take advantage of this woman's kindness.

CLARISSE: Reverend? I didn't know you was a Father. Now don't you worry about taking advantage of me. I'll let you know when you're taking advantage. If you ever do. Come on. Come on inside where it's warm.

THOMAS: Pardon me?

CLARISSE: We'll go up to my place for a bite first, okay? You look
             hungry. I've got some cold chicken. You can sing for
             your supper by saying grace. Are we living high
             tonight! (*she remembers the joint and lights up*) You
             could rest those sore tootsies too.

LENA: But what about Johnny?

CLARISSE: You got all night. The place doesn't start cooking for
             hours yet. And he can't see you like this, now can he?
             You're all messed up. Except for the necklace. I'll fix
             you up good first. Okay?

LENA: Okay.

CLARISSE: You want some?

LENA tokes too.

THOMAS: Wait a minute. Please.

CLARISSE: What is it, Father Tom?

THOMAS: Excuse me, but why are you doing this?

CLARISSE: Oh Reverend, you don't remember me, do you?

THOMAS: No. Are we related?

CLARISSE: We're both of us here for the same goddamn thing.
             Come on, you know what it is.

THOMAS: No. No, I don't recall.

CLARISSE: To serve mankind. To be the Good Samaritan. Us
              Indians got to help each other here in the big town.
              I'm going to help Lena here. And she can help me
              later. Do the dishes or something. That's fair, ain't it?

LENA: Sure thing.

THOMAS: I don't believe you.

CLARISSE: Here, sweetie, take the key. Go on, take it. I got to
              help the Rev along. You go ahead and put the kettle
              one. Number's on the key. It's the first building
              around the corner.

THOMAS: Lena, wait.

LENA: What's the matter now? You wanted someplace to
              rest. *(she exits)*

CLARISSE: Here, let me help you.

THOMAS: There's no need. Please don't—

CLARISSE: Do you know what you've got on your hands? Do you?

THOMAS: What are you talking about?

CLARISSE: You're a Reverend. Don't you know what an angel
              looks like? Open your eyes. She's in love. Do you
              know how rare that is? It's a precious thing. They
              don't make it much these days.

THOMAS: She's just an Indian girl in trouble.

CLARISSE: She's more than that, Reverend. She's real love in the flesh. Better than in the storybooks. I got to see what this guy looks like. I mean I don't usually hang out with my own kind. I usually steer clear. The drinking's okay, fun, but the fights! I mean I woke up with this shiner once, like I'd had an orgasm with my eye shadow, and shit, man, nobody'd come near me for weeks. Indians ain't good for business. And then they expect it for free. Do it for the Movement. Ha. I got a reputation, you know.

THOMAS: I don't know anything about it.

CLARISSE: If you say so. But don't she give you hope?

THOMAS: You don't know what you're talking about. You're blind to the light.

CLARISSE: I'm blind, eh? And I'm showing you the way. You're a chuckle. Come on. Let's go do our good deed. I'll fix your feet up so we can do the dip at the Dollar while we're at it.

CLARISSE leads THOMAS off.

Darkness. A telephone rings four times.

END OF ACT ONE

ACT TWO

ACT TWO, SCENE ONE

Darkness. A telephone rings four party line rings. A spot reveals it and LENA. She answers.

LENA: Hello. Hello. Is someone there?

JOHNNY'S
VOICE: Lena. Lena, is that you?

LENA: Who is this?

JOHNNY'S
VOICE: Oh Lena, babe, it's me.

LENA: Johnny. Johnny, what is it this time?

JOHNNY'S
VOICE: Oh babe, this city's the shits.

LENA: You been drinking.. You been drinking, haven't you? It's the middle of the night.

JOHNNY'S
VOICE: I can't take it, Lena. Shit, I can't take it no more.

LENA: You shouldn't be boozing it up.

JOHNNY'S
VOICE: You should come. I won't drink if you come.

LENA: A likely story.

JOHNNY'S VOICE:	You bitch. You bitch. You're as bad as your shitty sister.
LENA:	Johnny, I'm sorry. I'm sorry. I didn't mean it.

A dial tone starts and grows louder.

JOHNNY'S VOICE:	You'll be sorry, all right. You'll be sorry. I'll get myself killed.
LENA:	Don't talk crazy.
JOHNNY'S VOICE:	Don't talk crazy. That all you can say?
LENA:	I said I was sorry.
JOHNNY'S VOICE:	Sorry. Sorry. I'll make you sorry.
LENA:	Johnny, wait, wait, please. Don't hang up.
JOHNNY'S VOICE:	What I got to wait for? Tell me what I got to wait for.
LENA:	Johnny, be careful.
JOHNNY'S VOICE:	Be careful. You think I can't take care of myself.
LENA:	I don't know what I'd do if I lost you.

JOHNNY'S
VOICE: You already lost me, little girl.

LENA: Johnny, don't talk that way.

JOHNNY'S
VOICE: Didn't you hear? I started something at the Dollar.
                Some drunk used my own knife on me. The Swiss
                Army strikes again.

LENA: Johnny, that's not funny.

JOHNNY'S
VOICE: Not a belly laugh for sure. They keep on kicking at
                you, they're so drunk. Blood on their cowboy boots.
                Probably all your own fault.

The dial tone stops.

LENA: Johnny? Johnny, answer me. Where are you? Johnny?
                Johnny!

ACT TWO, SCENE TWO

A spot reveals BOO.

BOO: Come back here! Come back here, you creep! Oh
                shit.

*Another spot reveals MARTHA, flat on her back. MARTHA moans.
BOO turns and goes to her. The street appears.*

BOO: Oh Ma. Come on, get up. Come on. Upsy-daisy.
                Careful. You all right?

MARTHA: I'm not sure. I think so. Ow. Why you hit me?

BOO: You got stuff all over your behind.

MARTHA: I think I pulled something.

BOO: You'll survive. Well that's why you always tell me.

MARTHA: Where is it? Where's my purse?

BOO: That's what he knocked you down for.

MARTHA: How could he do that!

BOO: From where I was, it looked like one good tug.

MARTHA: Looked like an Indian boy too. Why would he do that
                to us?

BOO: I think we've arrived.

MARTHA: That's terrible, Boo. What will we do? Our tickets, our money.

BOO: We could call Aunty up.

MARTHA: No, I have to look for Lena.

BOO: She'd help. She's our family.

MARTHA: How can you tell? All that stuff that woman puts on her face, she looks like a corpse.

BOO: Ma, you're so tired.

MARTHA: I know how tired I am. Besides, your favourite aunt's probably busy.

BOO: You need to rest.

MARTHA: You won't find Lena by yourself.

BOO: I'd probably do better without having to be your body-guard.

MARTHA: I wish I'd come alone. Sometimes you're more trouble.

BOO: What's that supposed to mean?

MARTHA: Nothing. I just have to keep an eye on you or you'll upset your sister. All you do is argue.

BOO: I promise I won't upset her. Ma, I'll behave.

MARTHA: You upset Thomas too.

BOO: How do I upset the Rev?

MARTHA: You and your stupid pagan stories. He fears for your
            soul. *(she turns, exits down the street)*

BOO: *(to the light)* Ma, wait. Ma, come back. Ma, I worry
            about that stuff too.

            Ma, Coyote was alive once, alive, but this spirit who
            was dead showed Coyote the way to the land of the
            shadows. Ma, you see shadows everyday.

            They walked along for a long while over the plain,
            Coyote and the spirit. Then the spirit said, Oh look.
            That cloud of dust. Must be a herd of horses, eh? So
            Coyote agreed, Yes, there are a whole lot of horses.
            Even though you know he didn't see a one.

            Later that day, though the spirit knew Coyote couldn't
            see nothing, he said, Wow, look at all the berries.
            Let's have a bite before we go on. Just do like I do. So
            Coyote watched the spirit and imitated it, you know,
            putting his hand to his mouth as if he was eating
            berries, smacking his lips as if he had a mouth full of
            sweet juice, as if he was being fed.

ACT TWO, SCENE THREE

A telephone rings. A spot reveals THOMAS, shoeless on the edge of the couch. Another spot reveals CLARISSE, seated nearby on the floor, eating a sandwich from a plate.

CLARISSE: Let the thing ring.

THOMAS: You aren't going to answer it?

CLARISSE: The machine will take care of it.

The ringing stops.

THOMAS: It could be of some importance.

CLARISSE: Nah. Besides, I got visitors in from out of town, right? Can't you relax, Father Tom?

THOMAS: I want to offer you my thanks, dear lady.

CLARISSE: Clarisse. Call me by my name. Clarisse.

THOMAS: All right, my dear – Clarisse. I'm sorry I misjudged you. You've been an angel of mercy to us.

CLARISSE: You sure you don't want more to munch? You still look a bit wasted.

THOMAS: No. This will suffice. Clarisse. Thank you. It was an eventful drive.

CLARISSE: Can I get you something else, sweetie? You thirsty? How about something to drink?

THOMAS: No. No, thank you, dear lady – Clarisse.

CLARISSE: Lady Clarisse? I like that. Like hair lightener or some-
             thing? Ha. I wish you'd un-lax. I'm known for putting
             fellows at ease.

THOMAS: I apologize. I'm so concerned—

CLARISSE: Oh, she'll be okay. She was just hungry.

THOMAS: I don't think you understand, Clarisse.

CLARISSE: Just a couple of bruises on her arm. All she needs is a
             nap.

THOMAS: No, I'm not speaking of her flesh. It's her spiritual
             condition.

CLARISSE: Spiritual condition?

THOMAS: Lena isn't well. This young man she's after. Her mother
             and I are afraid she's possessed.

CLARISSE: Is that so? I don't think there's nothing wrong with
             being in love.

THOMAS: You don't understand, Clarisse. This Johnny. He came
             here alone a year ago and—

CLARISSE: A year! And they're still after each other's bods. That's
             great. That's adorable. Oh hell, I got to drink to that.
             You got to drink to that too. Come on. We both have
             to drink to that.

THOMAS: No, not for me, thank you.

CLARISSE: You sure?

THOMAS: Yes, nothing. Clarisse, please. About this Johnny she's looking for. The boy, he was killed six months ago. Yes. He's dead. Buried.

CLARISSE: Really? I guess you did your duty. The funeral?

THOMAS: Well, no. The remains were transported out west. That's where he was from.

CLARISSE: Where'd you say he bought it? Got killed.

THOMAS: The Silver Dollar.

CLARISSE: So that's why she's heading there?

THOMAS: Yes, he called her to come last night on the telephone.

CLARISSE: Really?

THOMAS: Yes, I'm afraid he's allianced with the evil one.

CLARISSE: That sure would fit.

THOMAS: It's more than I have strength for. I know that now after the accident. Clarisse, help me convince her to go back home.

CLARISSE: Her mother didn't like him?

THOMAS: Oh he was a wild boy. You know what they're like out west.

CLARISSE: Yeah, I do.

THOMAS: You must help me. Convince the child what madness
            this is. Her soul is in peril tonight. She almost destroyed
            our bodies today.

CLARISSE: That's real interesting, Reverend. I guess I could help.
            But you're going to have to tell me all about it. I don't
            have much spiritual experience. I'm not exactly a
            nun.

THOMAS: Let he who is without sin cast the first stone.

CLARISSE: I'll take that as a compliment. So come on. Let's drink
            to our partnership.

THOMAS: No, please, I don't drink.

CLARISSE: Don't drink? Really? Oh sweetie, you can't tell me
            that. I can see by looking at you that's not true. That
            nose almost glows in the dark.

THOMAS: No, please, Clarisse. I've given it up.

CLARISSE: Nobody ever gives it up. Reverend Tom, you have to
            down at least one. For luck. We'll need luck, won't
            we, to beat the devil?

THOMAS: I could use water or something.

CLARISSE: Oh you're not getting into the spirit of it.

THOMAS: No, thank you, dear lady. My flesh is weak.

CLARISSE: You're not that old, Tommy. I can tell. See. You've got
            reflexes. Oh relax. And look at this stuff. Come on.
            Better than holy water. You don't use that stuff, do

you? Here, take a sniff. Oh sorry. I didn't mean to. What a waster. You all right? I'll get a towel.

THOMAS: Never mind the towel. It dries fast.

CLARISSE: I'm sorry, Reverend.

THOMAS: It does smell good.

CLARISSE: All in a good cause. Against the devil. Here we go. There you are. Cheers.

THOMAS: Cheers.

CLARISSE: Okay. That went quick. Did we hit the spot or what? Clarisse knows what's good for the tired traveller. More? But we didn't do it right. We didn't toast to luck or whatever. It won't work unless we do it right.

THOMAS: No, please.

CLARISSE: Oh, come on.

CLARISSE tickles THOMAS.

CLARISSE: Come-on-come-on-come-on-come-on.

THOMAS: All right.

CLARISSE: Okay. Here we go. You make the toast. Wait a sec. Okay.

THOMAS: All right. May we defeat the evil that threatens the child Lena's soul. May we be victorious in the coming struggle. May the poor child find happiness and return—

CLARISSE: To Lena's happiness. So tell me details. Tell me about this nutso love affair. You said a whole year?

THOMAS: Her mother's very concerned.

CLARISSE: I've heard mothers can get like that. Did she hate his guts?

THOMAS: She was glad when the boy left, when he went away to work.

CLARISSE: Did Lena moon away over him?

THOMAS: Yes. She stayed in her bed for months. After he died. So many tears she shed. No one knew how to replenish her.

CLARISSE: I wish I could fall in love.

THOMAS: But this was like a disease, a madness. This is what it's like when the devil's involved. This is what he does to destroy our hope. Our boys kill themselves and our daughters act like...

CLARISSE: Would you call him a demon lover?

THOMAS: The boy was from out west. I hear they're still pagans out there. I suspected him from the start. I could see it in his eyes. A spirit like an animal's.

CLARISSE: I'll drink to that. Here. Let me fill you up.

THOMAS: Thanks. I didn't say anything about it. But I watched. I watched him close.

CLARISSE: I think I would too. Cheers.

THOMAS: I didn't want her worrying. But she couldn't help it, after the child got sick. I told her, Martha, be patient. All things come to those who wait.

CLARISSE: But what about the boy?

THOMAS: But Martha just worried, worried inside herself. Patience is a virtue, I told her.

CLARISSE: Heck, Reverend, I'm about to lose all what's left of my virtue. What about the sweethearts?

THOMAS: I said to Martha, We must pray. Let us pray for Lena.

CLARISSE: Come on, Tommy, tell me about Lena and Johnny.

THOMAS: And you know, she seemed to take some comfort in it. We got down on our knees and prayed. Heavenly Father, hallowed be Thy name.

CLARISSE: You're driving me to drink.

THOMAS: And I didn't mean to do it, but we were there, down on our knees together, praying, and I came to the knowing that my eyes were open and I was watching her lips moving as she prayed. I was drinking it in, the way her little pink tongue moved, making the words. I didn't care at all what she was saying. I didn't care at all.

CLARISSE: You got a crush on the old doll?

THOMAS: She trusted in me and in my heart I betrayed her.

CLARISSE: Oh, that's so sweet, Tommy.

THOMAS: My heart sank with shame inside my chest.

CLARISSE: Oh. come off it, Reverend. What's the big problem? It's adorable.

THOMAS: We were praying for her daughter. For her poor daughter's soul.

CLARISSE: Reverend Tommy, Lena's a big girl. She can take care of herself.

THOMAS: And all I could feel – lust. Lust. I wanted to die.

CLARISSE: You're just a guy, Tommy. Just a man.

CLARISSE kisses THOMAS' cheek.

THOMAS: Don't do that.

CLARISSE: What's the matter?

THOMAS: You shouldn't do that to me.

CLARISSE: You unclean? Oh cheer up, Tommy. It don't mean a thing. Not a thing.

THOMAS: Only a whore could say that. Only a whore.

CLARISSE: I'm not arguing with you, Reverend.

THOMAS: I'm – thirsty. Clarisse, do you hear? I'm thirsty.

CLARISSE: You've had enough.

THOMAS: Give me that.

CLARISSE: No more 'til you settle down. You got to tell me more about—

THOMAS: Give it to me!

CLARISSE: Ow! Don't you think you should slow down a bit?

THOMAS: I'm thirsty. And this hits the spot. What kind of a whore are you, anyway? I'm the one who's supposed to say what's sin.

CLARISSE: It's okay with you, it must be okay, I guess.

THOMAS: It's okay with me, lady, okay by me. God, I been thirsty. Look at it. Look at that colour. Like dawn. Hey, where you going? You're not going to leave me high and dry, pretty lady? Lady Clarisse.

CLARISSE: Guess not. Guess I could stay a little bit longer.

THOMAS: A little bit longer? Hell, woman, what kind of a whore are you? You're supposed to be in service, in service to the devil.

CLARISSE: Listen, Reverend, I don't do charity work.

THOMAS: You're pulling me down, you're making me fall.

CLARISSE: Back off, Reverend. Back off.

THOMAS: Come on, whore, whore of the city of darkness.Come
            on. Just a little kiss. Give me some tongue.

CLARISSE: Sorry, Father. No pay, no play.

THOMAS: Oh, what a temptress you are. What a red woman, an
            evil woman.

CLARISSE: You're really into this, aren't you?

THOMAS: Lady. Pretty lady. Pretty Lady Clarisse. Handmaid of
            Darkness.

CLARISSE: Oh brother. Here. Here's the extra bottle.

THOMAS: Thank you, Dark Lady. Thank you.

CLARISSE exits.

THOMAS: It's a beautiful colour. Light in a bottle. This is to you,
            Lady Clarisse. It hits the spot. To you.

ACT TWO, SCENE FOUR

A spot. BOO and MARTHA wander into it.

MARTHA: Boo. Boo, I don't like this place. Why are the lights all off?

BOO: It's a bar. It's atmosphere.

MARTHA: It is smoky in here. You think Lena's here someplace?

BOO: That's what she said.

MARTHA: But all they do here is drink.

BOO: I can't see them nowhere. Come on. Here's a seat.

MARTHA: Let's go. We can wait for them outside.

BOO: Ma, you're so tired, you're almost falling down. In here at least we can get off our feet. Come on.

MARTHA: They'll want us to drink.

BOO: What's a couple of draft? I could use one.

MARTHA: We don't have money.

BOO: I've got a few bucks in my pocket. Sit down. Sit down, Ma, please.

MARTHA: Oh, all right. But I don't like it, Boo. It's so crowded.

BOO: Ma, there's hardly nobody here yet.

MARTHA: Daughter, tell me the truth. You've been here before?

BOO: Of course I have.

MARTHA: What were you doing here?

BOO: Having some beer. With friends. From school.

MARTHA: But this is an awful place. I didn't bring you up like
            that. Who are they all?

BOO: They're just people, Ma. Lots of Indians. Look
            around.

MARTHA: I don't see nobody I know. And it's so dark. Why
            would anybody in their right mind come here?

BOO: So just where the hell else are they going to go, Ma?
            They ain't rich.

MARTHA: You watch your tongue, Daughter.

BOO: I'm sorry, Ma. Just relax. I'll go get the draft.

ACT TWO, SCENE FIVE

A spot reveals LENA, awake in bed, a blanket pulled around her.
CLARISSE enters.

CLARISSE: Hiya.

LENA: Hi.

CLARISSE: You're awake?

LENA: I did sleep. I didn't think I was sleepy.

CLARISSE: Clarisse knows what's good for the tired traveller.

LENA: I dreamed something strange about Johnny.

CLARISSE: God, you got it bad, don't you?

LENA: Is it late? I can't keep him waiting.

CLARISSE: Don't worry. You won't keep him long. We'll get ready.
              Let's wash that face.

LENA: Where's the Reverend?

CLARISSE: Having a snooze. Don't worry about him. Take off the
              blouse.

LENA: He wasn't rude, was he? Sometimes he gets preach-
              ing.

CLARISSE: He sure does. He's a funny old fuck. Pretty harmless,
              though. What I'm worried about is you looking your
              best for your reunion.

LENA: You're very good to us. To me.

CLARISSE: Yeah, I am, aren't I? Sister'd be proud of me today.

LENA: You got a sister?

CLARISSE: Nuns taught me how to count.

LENA: Oh. I just got a regular sister.

CLARISSE: You didn't miss nothing, baby. Hand me that towel.

LENA: My sister, she came to the city to school.

CLARISSE: I didn't learn nothing 'til I got out of school. What
             they call real life.

LENA: My sister don't know about real life. She's so young.
             You know all about real life, don't you?

CLARISSE: Hey, I'm not that old.

LENA: But you know about boys. I mean men.

CLARISSE: Yeah, I know about them. Boy, do I know boys. What
             is it?

LENA: Johnny. He's real special to me.

CLARISSE: I can see it when you say his name. Your eyes get a
             light inside them. Come over to the mirror.

LENA: It's all a little crazy.

CLARISSE: Crazy, yeah. Tell me about it. Sit. Sit.

LENA: I never felt like this about a boy before.

CLARISSE: You're blushing. I forgot girls could do that.

LENA: You know what I mean? This feeling.

CLARISSE: You got goosebumps just talking about him.

LENA: Sometimes I don't know where I end no more.

CLARISSE: Oh. you got it. You got the glow. Oh, it must be sweet. Is he good to you?

LENA: Sure thing. But it's scary when he's not here.

CLARISSE: Scary? How's that?

LENA: I'm afraid he'll stop loving me, Clarisse.

CLARISSE: Oh sweetie, don't say that. Even if it's true. Don't think about it. Not yet.

LENA: I don't want him to stop loving me. Not ever.

CLARISSE: Kid, love don't come with a guarantee.

LENA: It has to be perfect.

CLARISSE: All you can do is go with the flow.

LENA: It's going to be perfect. I won't lose him, Clarisse. I won't.

CLARISSE: I don't think you'll have to. Princess, you're beautiful.

LENA: I'm just ordinary. But you can show me what to do.

CLARISSE: What I know. I don't know if it's what you want.

LENA: Show me, Clarisse. Show me what to do.

CLARISSE: Okay. Okay, I will. This necklace is a good start. Wait a sec. Here. I've been saving this for a special occasion. Saving it for too long. I bet it fits you.

LENA: It's beautiful.

CLARISSE: It sure stops traffic all right. See the cut. This'll show him you mean business.

LENA: I don't know. Can I wear that?

CLARISSE: Of course you can. If you can't, nobody can. You got a beautiful body.

LENA: I've never worn nothing like that before.

CLARISSE: You're in love. You never been in love before either, right? Come on. This looks like love like nothing else.

LENA: But he's never seen me in nothing but blue jeans.

CLARISSE: In this you'll be his red red rose. If that don't keep him loving you, I don't know. This is what I know, Princess.

LENA: A rose? A rose. Okay.

CLARISSE: Okay! Throw those blues away. Just a sec. Let's see. These heels should fit. And these stockings too.

LENA: Oh Clarisse, my goosebumps are back.

CLARISSE: Like magic, eh? Come on. Sit down. This is the way
            to live. Oh baby, you got beautiful hair. Black as night.
            You won't need perfume.

LENA: That hurts.

CLARISSE: Sorry. It's so thick. You could drown in it. A couple of
            knots. There. There. Let's do your puss now.

LENA: What is that, that stuff?

CLARISSE: This stuff? It's something to keep you blushing all
            night long.

LENA: It feels funny. Do we really need it?

CLARISSE: Oh relax, Princess. I usually just think of it as war-
            paint. What's the matter?

LENA: I look so different.

CLARISSE: When I'm done, you'll be beautiful. Just a touch. You
            don't need much. A touch. Your own mother won't
            know her baby girl. There. Yeah. Yeah. What do you
            say?

LENA: That's me?

CLARISSE: That's you. You could be a pro. The Foxy Lady.

LENA: I don't know. He won't know it's me.

CLARISSE:	Oh. come on. Don't worry. He'll know you. He wants you. You'll knock him dead. Careful. You're smudging it.
LENA:	I'm sorry. He didn't call, did he? While I was asleep?
CLARISSE:	No, of course not. How could he?
LENA:	Something's happened. Oh Clarisse, something's happened to him.
CLARISSE:	Sweetie, calm down. Calm down.
LENA:	While I was sleeping. He died. I know it. While I was sleeping.
CLARISSE:	No, sweetie, no. Don't be silly. No tears now. Calm down. Calm down. He's okay. He's waiting for you at the Dollar. Everything's cool.
LENA:	Do you think – was it a dream?
CLARISSE:	Yeah, that's it. A nightmare. That's all it was. Just a silly imagining. You're just excited. About seeing him.
LENA:	Yeah, that's it.
CLARISSE:	You shouldn't listen to that crazy Reverend.
LENA:	It was just a dream. It's been too long.
CLARISSE:	How long has it been?
LENA:	I can't remember. Why can't I remember?

CLARISSE: It's been one of those days, Princess.

LENA: One of those days. Yeah.

CLARISSE: Hold still. It'll come to you. I got to touch up that eye.

LENA: He's been here – it's a year.

CLARISSE: That is a long time.

LENA: He wanted to earn enough so we could get married.

CLARISSE: You didn't want to shack up?

LENA: He had to prove he was good enough. He said my Momma didn't like him. He works for Aunty's husband. Aunty's husband's a lawyer.

CLARISSE: Sounds promising. Lawyers can be generous. Pout those lips. That's right. What about you? A year's a long time.

LENA: He said he'd visit. I guess it's so far.

CLARISSE: Out in the bush?

LENA: Me and my sister and my Momma. And lots of bush.

CLARISSE: Here. Lips like this.

LENA: It takes forever to get to our place. The road's so bad. We got the last old log house down by the river.

CLARISSE: Is it as boring as it sounds?

LENA: My sister says the one excitement's when the river
             floods. We have to move to the attic.

CLARISSE: That where you want to live? In the attic?

LENA: No way.

CLARISSE: A little log cabin. Kind of sounds like a little bit of
             paradise. Just the pair of you. Come on. Arms up over
             your head.

LENA: He has been saving his money. He's on the wagon.

CLARISSE: Okay. Pull in the tumtum.

LENA: When he sees me – it's a little tight. It's hard to
             breathe.

CLARISSE: Well, maybe. But you're light-headed anyway.

LENA: Yeah. He called last night.

CLARISSE: And you're going to give it a shot. Hell, you deserve to
             hit the spot. These earrings. Here. They should be
             the finishing touch.

LENA: They're like stars, aren't they?

CLARISSE: Yeah. That's the spirit. Oh yeah. Look at yourself. See.
             Look. What do you think? What do you think your
             Johnny will think?

ACT TWO, SCENE SIX

Darkness.

JOHNNY: This place is really big. Really big. Humungous. Your woman, she's inside of here somewhere. Just wait outside here while I go in and look around for her. *(in a spot and to the light)* My granddad, he'd stop here, you know, all the time, letting us get the picture, Shadow Man and Coyote there at the door to the lodge of the dead. The Lodge of the Dead! Shit, it used to freak me out, man. A big building made out of the darkest parts of the night. My little heart beat away like nothing. The old guy was a card. The way he told it, I don't know, he made us see it, Coyote and this shadow guy in the middle of nowhere, sitting out there, eating dust, pretending to be in some lodge with Coyote's dead wife. *(his spot begins to fade)* And then, just like that, the sun goes down. And there they are, people all around him.

Another spot begins to reveal BOO.

JOHNNY: Coyote hears them folks whispering at first and then really talking. All of them living their lives in the land of the dead. And the ghost of his wife, shit, she'd been there all along, sitting by his side. She's cooking him a rabbit stew or something for his supper. *(his spot goes out)*

MARTHA: That man, Boo. That man.

The spot on BOO reveals MARTHA too.

BOO: What man?

MARTHA: That man over there. He's looking at me.

BOO: Oh yeah. Well, don't look back. Or do you like it?

MARTHA: I won't have you talking to me that way. I won't.

BOO: I didn't mean nothing.

MARTHA: That's your trouble. You never mean nothing.

BOO: Ma, what's that supposed to mean?

MARTHA: Nothing. Drink your draft.

BOO: Ma, you must mean something.

MARTHA: The way you been acting all day. Like you're on holiday.

BOO: Ma, I'm here, aren't I?

MARTHA: You're here. And what are you up to? Drinking. Drinking beer. And smoking. How's that supposed to help your sister?

BOO: It helps pass the time.

MARTHA: I don't want you ordering any more of those things. Not another. I want you ready to go soon as your sister comes in. I want you sober. You hear me?

BOO: Yeah, Ma. Ma, she don't show soon, I think we should phone the cops.

MARTHA: No. Don't be stupid, Boo. You know what they'll do to her.

BOO: Oh Ma, that's crazy.

MARTHA: Don't you dare tell me I'm crazy. Don't you dare.

BOO: I'm sorry, Ma. I said I'm sorry.

MARTHA: Well, so you should be. This whole thing's all your fault.

BOO: What are you talking about?

MARTHA: You introduced your sister to him. Why you'd bring a boy like that home I'll never know.

BOO: I wanted to talk to him, Ma.

MARTHA: Talk? What could you two talk about so much?

BOO: Oh, he knew things, Ma. About the world

MARTHA: Him? Boo, what good does it do? You're nobody who matters.

BOO: Thanks a lot, Ma.

MARTHA: Boo, you matter to me. I'm your mother. But to waste your life on useless things.

BOO: They weren't useless to me, Ma.

MARTHA: Oh Boo, why do you act like that? Why are you so bad?

BOO: Bad! Am I the one who went boozing and screwing around the countryside last summer?

MARTHA: Watch your tongue. It wasn't like that at all.

BOO: So how was it? How was it?

MARTHA: It was beautiful. Your sister was so happy, happier than you'll ever know.

BOO: Drunk without even drinking draft.

MARTHA: She wasn't drunk.

BOO: She was too, Ma.

MARTHA: She was in love.

BOO: Love! Ma, listen. She's got a date with a dead man. She's out of her head.

MARTHA: She's not out of her head. Don't say that.

BOO: Well, how else would you say it? That's what this whole Johnny thing's about.

MARTHA: Boo, it was an accident, an accident. It didn't have to happen this way.

BOO: They could be living happily ever after today?

MARTHA: Yes, of course they could.

BOO: You didn't know Johnny.

MARTHA: Who wanted to? All that bad language out of his mouth. All that filth.

BOO: And you let us go around with him?

MARTHA: Lena was so happy at first. I didn't know how bad he was.

BOO: Lena was happy. Lena. Well, what about me?

MARTHA: Oh you. You can take care of yourself.

BOO: Thanks, Ma. Thanks a lot. Where the hell are they?

MARTHA: Why do you have to talk like that?

BOO: Look, Ma. He's still there. Just imagine. If the Rev hadn't found the Lord, that could be him today.

MARTHA: Don't be smart.

ACT TWO, SCENE SEVEN

Darkness. A telephone rings.

THOMAS: Who's there? Who's there? *(a spot reveals him sprawled on the couch)* Hell. A man could die of thirst around here. Hello. Anybody there? Hello. My mouth's dry. Oh Lord, where's everybody?

Ah ha. This should hit the spot. The spot. Lady Clarisse. Clarisse. Oh no. Emptiness. Emptiness.

Oh Heavenly Father, give me your strength. I have stumbled again into the wilderness. I'm lost. Again. Help me find my way out of this darkness. Help me, Lord, please. Supply your servant with a light. Oh Father in – Lena. Where's Lena? Lena! Lena! Where are you? Oh, your mother's going to kill me now. *(he pulls on his shoes)*

ACT TWO, SCENE EIGHT

Spots reveal the street. LENA and CLARISSE enter.

LENA: Is that it? Those flashing lights?

CLARISSE: That's it, Princess. The old Buck.

LENA: The Silver Dollar. Come on.

CLARISSE: Just a sec, sweetie. We don't want to blow it. Let's just go over it once more.

LENA: I know what to do now.

CLARISSE: Princess, the Boy Scout motto. It don't hurt to be prepared.

LENA: Oh all right. It does have to go perfect.

CLARISSE: That's my sweetie. Here. Check your makeup.

LENA: Is it okay? I don't know about that stuff.

CLARISSE: You'll have to learn how to do yourself one day. But that stuff is great, if I do say so myself. But don't smile like that. Shows your gums. Remember what I told you.

LENA: Save the eyes and the teeth for the kill?

CLARISSE: Right. Here. Just a little bit more lip stuff.

LENA: It doesn't sound right to me.

CLARISSE: He'll love it. It's exciting. Keep still. Ah, that does it. God, you're beautiful. I'd kiss you myself but I don't want to muss it up.

LENA: Let's go. Come on.

CLARISSE: Just remember the number one rule. No love talk.

LENA: But I do love him.

CLARISSE: But it breaks the spell, Princess.

LENA: I don't know. I guess so.

CLARISSE: Follow his lead. Let him do most of the talking. Men like to hear themselves talk. Makes them think they got an audience. Understand?

LENA: He does have an audience.

CLARISSE: Don't go all puddly now. Don't you want to take him by the hand and lead him home to your little log cabin paradise?

LENA: He's waiting, Clarisse.

CLARISSE: Princess, do me a favour? Let me go in ahead. Give me a minute or two to get a brew and a seat. I want to watch the way you come into that dump. And don't you even say Hi to me again if he's already there. You shouldn't be bothering with anyone else tonight. I just want to watch the two of you together. Hold it a minute or two just for me.

LENA: You want to watch us.

CLARISSE: I want to see all my hard work work out.

LENA: I guess that's fair.

They hug.

ACT TWO, SCENE NINE

Spots reveal BOO and MARTHA.

BOO: Ma, I'm going to the ladies'.

MARTHA: Boo, wait. Maybe I should come with you.

BOO: I can take care of myself! I mean somebody's got to watch my sweater. *(she exits)*

MARTHA: Boo, wait.

Oh, where is she? It can't take this long to go to the ladies'.

CLARISSE enters.

CLARISSE: Hiya, lady. Mind if I sit here?

MARTHA: No, I'm saving it. I'm sorry. Please, you can't sit there.

CLARISSE: But lady, there's no more chairs left.

MARTHA: But I'm saving this seat for my daughter.

CLARISSE: This won't take long. I'll keep it warm for her, okay?

MARTHA: She's just gone to the ladies' room.

CLARISSE: She'll be gone forever. There's always a line. Look, I'll move soon as she gets back. Okay? Okay?

MARTHA: I suppose that's all right.

CLARISSE: Okay. Let me tell you, lady, you're going to see something real special here tonight. It'll make you feel young again.

MARTHA: My age is none of your business.

CLARISSE: I'm sorry. Can I buy you a beer? Come on. You're almost empty. Let me buy you a draft.

MARTHA: I can buy my own draft.

CLARISSE: If you say so. Hey, waiter, two more all around.

MARTHA: But I don't want one.

CLARISSE: Don't worry about it. I'll drink yours. I'm celebrating the return of lost love.

ACT TWO, SCENE TEN

A spot reveals BOO.

BOO: Can I use that sink now? Thanks.

Oh. Feels good. My eyes were stinging. Shit, they're red. Looks like I'm the one who's been crying for six months. Shit.

Another spot starts to reveal JOHNNY.

BOO: Lena. What did he do to you to make you go cuckoo? He was an all right guy but I guess there's no accounting for taste. Shit, John Boy, what did you do to my Big Sister?

JOHNNY: Shit! Shit. Does her mother know she talks like that? Does your mother know you talk like that?

BOO: What you been saying to my sister? You turned my Big Sister into a Cry Baby.

JOHNNY: You know me, Boo. Four letter words. Love-love-love-love.

BOO: You leave her alone. All you want to do is fuck. You don't love nobody.

JOHNNY: You don't love nobody.

BOO: Shit.

JOHNNY: Shit! That all you can say?

BOO: That's all you can say.

JOHNNY: So how come you like to hear me say it?

BOO: So maybe I like the way you say it. I never heard
            nobody make so much out of a little bit of shit before.

JOHNNY: A likely story?

BOO: But I do like the way you tell it.

JOHNNY: Shit. It's a stupid story. It don't mean nothing.

BOO: Maybe it's you I like telling it.

JOHNNY: Shit. Shit on maybe. Shit on telling it. Shit on—

BOO: Shit?

JOHNNY: Shit. Coyote shit.

            So, this guy Coyote's spending every nighttime there
            in the big lodge of the shadow people. His wife's
            there too and all his old gang. A wild old time it is.
            They talk and laugh and eat and play games for hours.
            Poker probably. And everyday for days in the daytime
            he has to wait, sitting out there in that desert place
            on the plain, all alone in the hot sun, almost dying too
            with nothing to drink, just so he could visit for another
            night with his wife.

            How come we never had a night together?

BOO: Oh John Boy, I did like you. I just – Johnny?

JOHNNY: Boo?

BOO: What are you doing here?

JOHNNY: What are you doing here?

BOO: .   Johnny, I— you— Shit, Johnny this is the ladies'.

JOHNNY: So that's why you're here. So how you doing? What is
             this? The Boo speechless? I should have caught her
             in the can before.

BOO: It's just I think I got a lot of stuff to say to you. I mean,
             shit, Johnny, what's it like where you are?

ACT TWO, SCENE ELEVEN

The spot reveals MARTHA and CLARISSE.

CLARISSE: Hey lady, look.

MARTHA: What is it now?

CLARISSE: Look at that girl.

MARTHA: What? Where?

CLARISSE: Over there. Near the door. See? Ain't she a beauty?

MARTHA: She looks like my Lena.

CLARISSE: What did you say?

MARTHA: She looks like Lena.

CLARISSE: How did you know her name?

MARTHA: But something's wrong with her face.

CLARISSE: There's nothing wrong with her. That's the way they like them nowadays.

MARTHA: It is Lena.

CLARISSE: Of course it's Lena.

MARTHA: I have to talk to her. Let me by.

CLARISSE: No, wait, lady, wait.

MARTHA: I have to go talk to her.

CLARISSE: Couldn't it wait? She's here to meet somebody. Somebody special.

MARTHA: What do you know about it? I'm her mother.

CLARISSE: Be a sweetie, Momma. You'll cramp her style.

MARTHA: Let me out.

CLARISSE: Come on, Momma. Give love a chance.

MARTHA: Who are you? Get away. Oh no, she's gone.

CLARISSE: I'm not telling.

MARTHA: Oh my God! Is that Thomas?

CLARISSE: You know that nut?

MARTHA: What's he doing?

CLARISSE: I thought he was out for the night.

MARTHA: He must see her. He does. He does see her! Good. Good, he'll stop her.

CLARISSE: Does nobody love love around here? *(she exits)*

MARTHA: Wait a minute.

ACT TWO, SCENE TWELVE

A spot reveals LENA.

LENA: *(to the light)* Johnny. Johnny, is that you? I'm here, Johnny. See me. I want you to look at me. All these people. They're looking at me. They think I'm pretty. But that's not the same. All those eyes and nobody really sees. Johnny, please answer me. I know you're here. Come on. Come to me. *(she dances for the light)*

THOMAS: Lena! Wait, child!

LENA: I'm beautiful for you, Johnny. *(her spot goes out)*

A spot reveals THOMAS.

THOMAS: Lena! Lena. Where'd she go?

CLARISSE enters with drinks.

CLARISSE: Coming through. Coming through. How you doing, Reverend Tom?

THOMAS: Lena – the girl was just here.

CLARISSE: Hold still a sec, Reverend. Look what I got for you.

THOMAS: I must not lose her again.

CLARISSE: Catch your breath. You're shaking all over. Here you go. Hair of the dog.

THOMAS: Please, I can't. Her mother would be most disap-pointed if—

CLARISSE: Who's going to tell her? Come on, come on. Lena's a big girl, isn't she? Isn't she? Let her alone.

THOMAS: But the devil is here. Something may happen to her.

CLARISSE: Oh I think you're the one who needs protection. Come on over here. Come on along.

THOMAS: But I'm her guardian.

CLARISSE: Don't you worry about her. Come on. Take it. Come on. That's it. Good, ain't it? Her Momma knows all about it anyway.

THOMAS: What's that? What are you saying?

CLARISSE: There's nothing you can do about it. Her Momma's here right now, looking for her.

THOMAS: She's here?

CLARISSE: Yeah. Over there someplace. I had a nip with the old girl.

THOMAS: Martha does not nip.

CLARISSE: I was trying to be delicate. It's a joke, okay?

THOMAS: She is here? And she's seen the thing you done to her daughter?

CLARISSE: I suppose you could do better?

THOMAS: Where is she? Where is she? Can you see her?

CLARISSE: Hey now, hey. Take it easy. Sit down.

THOMAS: I am dead now. I am. I know she'll never look at me
              again. I'm sinking into hell.

CLARISSE: Hey, come on now, cheer up. Nothing's that bad.

THOMAS: I'm in hell. I'm in hell now.

CLARISSE: You must be really thirsty then. Come on. Drink up.
              Come on. That's it. Clarisse'll fix everything.

ACT TWO, SCENE THIRTEEN

A spot reveals MARTHA.

MARTHA: *(to the dark)* Have you seen my little girl? My daughter Lena. She's run away from home. No, no thanks. I don't drink. Lena, she's very pretty. A very pretty girl. A very good girl. You'd know her if you saw her. You'd remember. You know how girls get. A boy, a wild boy. She's here somewhere. I just saw her a few minutes ago. Over there? A pretty girl? Oh, thanks. I'll see. I'll try. Thanks a lot.

ACT TWO, SCENE FOURTEEN

Spots reveal BOO and JOHNNY.

JOHNNY: Buy me a drink.

BOO: Johnny, you can't drink.

JOHNNY: Come on, Boo, I haven't had one forever.

BOO: You know what you said your granddad said about spirits.

JOHNNY: I'm dying of thirst, Boo. I can't get a drink in this shitty place.

BOO: That's just the point, Johnny. The dying bit?

JOHNNY: I don't need no lecture, Boo. You're not my granddad. What I need is a drink.

BOO: John Boy, there's a reason no one will serve you.

JOHNNY: It's because I'm an Indian.

BOO: This time it's bigger than that.

JOHNNY: Your Big Sister lectured me the last time I called her. The chick's got no sense of humour.

BOO: Listen to me, Johnny.

JOHNNY: I'm good for it. I'll pay you back.

BOO: How the hell are you good for it? How you going to pay?

JOHNNY: I got a job.

BOO: You? What is it? Prove it. What's this job?

JOHNNY: I get chicks to buy me beer. I tell them how cute they are. I let them touch me.

BOO: Come on, Johnny, when's the last time anybody touched you? When you touched the wrong guy's girl friend? Is that how it happened?

JOHNNY: I give them what they need. I even been known to tell them some stories. I'm good at telling stories.

BOO: Shit. You don't believe a word of it. I got one to tell you, John Boy.

JOHNNY: For a beer? Where you want me to start?

BOO: I said I'm telling it to you this time.

Coyote and his wife, they were living together. Living together like happiness. Then his wife got sick, so sick she died. She was dead. And Coyote got very lonesome, John Boy, so lonesome he didn't do a thing but drink. He drank for his wife.

JOHNNY: Wait a minute.

BOO: Who's telling it?

JOHNNY: You. You are, Boo.

ACT TWO, SCENE FIFTEEN

A spot reveals THOMAS and CLARISSE dancing together clumsily.

THOMAS: Where you been all my life? Light of my life.

CLARISSE: You're a card, Rev.

THOMAS: A card? What you mean?

CLARISSE: A joker.

THOMAS: Oh yeah. Well, you, my dear Lady Clarisse, are a queen.

CLARISSE: Well, don't step on our royal toes, okay?

THOMAS: You are the Queen of Hearts, of my heart.

CLARISSE: Oh, you fickle thing.

THOMAS: Let's toast it. Come on, toast again.

CLARISSE: Shouldn't we be taking it easier about now?

THOMAS: To hell with easy. I'm in love.

CLARISSE: Okay, then. To hell with easy. To love.

ACT TWO, SCENE SIXTEEN

A spot reveals MARTHA and LENA.

MARTHA: Daughter! Lena, it's me.

LENA: Momma, what you doing here?

MARTHA: What am I doing here! I'm half dead worrying.

LENA: Momma, go away.

MARTHA: You can't take care of yourself.

LENA: I'm here for Johnny.

MARTHA: Lena, get that nonsense out of your head. Your sister and I travelled all day for you.

LENA: Boo? Boo's here too? Momma, I'm a grown-up.

MARTHA: You look it. What's that stuff on your face?

LENA: No, Momma, don't.

MARTHA: Nonsense. That's what it is. I almost didn't know you.

LENA: Momma, please, it's for Johnny.

MARTHA: Johnny! He wouldn't know you like this. Let's clean it off.

LENA: He would too.

MARTHA: And where are your own clothes? This is indecent.

LENA: Leave me alone. Leave me alone! Get away from me!

MARTHA is knocked to the floor as LENA pulls away and exits.

MARTHA: Lena, wait! Daughter, wait! I'm your mother.

ACT TWO, SCENE SEVENTEEN

Spots reveal JOHNNY and BOO.

BOO: He partied, John Boy, Coyote partied with all his old
            friends who had passed over. There in that longhouse
            all night long they were together again around the
            fire. People brought him drinks.

JOHNNY: You tell it almost like my granddad, Boo. Shit, you
            really see it. You believe that shit!

BOO: The spirit guide finally said—

JOHNNY: Hey Coyote, the time has come. You can go now,
            leave the land of the dead. You can take your wife
            home with you. Back to the land of the living. I warn
            you, though—

BOTH: Don't you touch her. She has to be completely alive
            again. She has to be wholly flesh again—

BOO: I will do exactly as you say, Coyote said. But you know
            Coyote—

BOTH: It went right through his head!

A spot reveals LENA.

LENA: I got to check my face.

BOO: Lena?

LENA: Get out of my way. I need the mirror. I – what are you
            doing in here?

JOHNNY: Keep telling about Coyote, Boo.

LENA: Johnny? Johnny, I'm here.

JOHNNY: Go on, Boo. What's stopping you?

LENA: Johnny, it's me.

JOHNNY: What happened next?

LENA: It's this stuff. I'll take it off.

JOHNNY: Shit, I like the way you tell it.

BOO: So Coyote and his wife, they headed off across the plain. And at first she was nothing but a shadow.

LENA: Look, Johnny. I've cleaned it off.

BOO: At night, when they had made camp, they would sit and talk about their life to come. And Coyote would look at his wife and there were lights again in her black hair and even in the shadows where her eyes were.

JOHNNY: You ever love someone like that, Boo? Enough to bring them back?

BOO: No. Not me. How about you?

LENA: Johnny, Johnny, look at me.

JOHNNY: I can't remember nobody. No, me neither. But that place can't be all that bad. Shit, they do party there too.

BOO: Coyote sat up in the dark and reached out. He pulled his wife into his arms and kissed her.

LENA: Shut up, Boo. That has nothing to do with us.

BOO: And Coyote's wife turned into smoke, turned back to the land of the dead.

JOHNNY: Can't kiss you goodbye.

LENA: Johnny, what about me? Johnny, I love you. I love you.

JOHNNY: *(he turns to go)* See you around. *(his spot goes out)*

LENA: Please, at least look at me.

BOO: Come on, Lena.

LENA: Leave me alone. Johnny, Johnny, come back here. I came all this way for you. *(she exits)*

BOO: Lena, Big Sister, wait.

ACT TWO, SCENE EIGHTEEN

*A spot reveals THOMAS and CLARISSE, still dancing. MARTHA
enters.*

MARTHA: Thomas. Thomas!

THOMAS: What's that? Who's there, Clarisse?

CLARISSE: It's your old flame. You know, the tongue lady?

THOMAS: Martha? Dear Martha, come dance with us.

MARTHA: Thomas, how could you do it?

THOMAS: Come, my dear, let's celebrate. Love has returned.

MARTHA: How could you let that happen to Lena?

THOMAS: Lena? Lena's a big girl. The Queen here attests to the
               fact.

MARTHA: I trusted you with her.

THOMAS: I did take care of her. Didn't I take care of her?

MARTHA: You disgust me. Never again. You're just a drunk old
               Indian.

CLARISSE: Come on, lady, lighten up.

MARTHA: I was stupid to think you were anything better. Rever-
               end! You belong in the gutter. I hope you go back
               there. Nursing you back to life was a waste of time.

	You're a drunk. You make me ashamed, ashamed to be Indian.
THOMAS:	Martha, I apologize. I'm deeply sorry.
MARTHA:	Get away. You're a disgrace.
THOMAS:	Please. I did my best. The devil is so strong here. Say you forgive me.
MARTHA:	The devil! You old fool. She hit me. Hit me! Do you know that? Lena hit me. It's all your fault.
CLARISSE:	Come on, lady. That's nobody's fault. The girl's in love. Let her grow up.
MARTHA:	Love? Love! You don't know what you're talking about. My daughter is sick.
CLARISSE:	Love is not a sickness.
MARTHA:	She's chasing a ghost. A boy who was murdered here six months ago.
CLARISSE:	Wait a minute. You believe that shit too.
MARTHA:	Her Johnny died here. A knife fight. Drunk Indians. Blood and drunk Indians. Oh, I hate this place. He's dead. Dead and buried and gone to hell for all I care.
CLARISSE:	So that shit's all true? She can't be crazy. She's so beautiful.
THOMAS:	Martha, I beg you. In your heart, forgive me.

MARTHA: Get away. You're an animal.

THOMAS: I wanted to marry you. I wanted to be a father to your daughters.

MARTHA: You're so sad. You can't even take care of yourself.

THOMAS: I love you.

MARTHA: Get away. You don't know what love is. I pity you. I pity you both. Let go of me. Let go.

CLARISSE: Come on, Tommy. Take it easy. Let her go. She ain't worth it. Come on. Tommy? Tommy? Shit, lady, something's wrong.

MARTHA: Get him away from me.

CLARISSE: Lady, I think it's his ticker.

MARTHA: He can go to hell for all I care. Go to hell.

CLARISSE: Lady, I think he's dead.

MARTHA: Do you know what he did to my daughter? Go to hell.

CLARISSE: Lady, lady, the old fuck's dead.

MARTHA: Don't be stupid. He's drunk.

CLARISSE: Shit, lady, dead drunk. This is the limit. I'm out of here. (*she exits*)

MARTHA: Get up. Get up, you fool. Thomas? Thomas? You old fool. She hit me. You know that? Right here. Lena hit me. *(she kicks at him)*

ACT TWO, SCENE NINETEEN

A spot reveals fleeing CLARISSE. LENA intercepts her.

LENA: Clarisse, where you going?

CLARISSE: I got to get out of here.

LENA: You can't go now. I need your help.

CLARISSE: I don't want no trouble with the cops. And your friend the Rev just dropped dead.

LENA: Clarisse, Johnny was here.

CLARISSE: He was, was he?

LENA: He wouldn't look at me.

CLARISSE: Yeah, well, surprise, surprise. What you done to yourself?

LENA: I was afraid he wouldn't know me. I looked so different.

CLARISSE: Kid, nobody'd know you, the mess it is now.

LENA: I'm sorry. I should have listened. Fix me up.

CLARISSE: I can't hang around here.

LENA: You got to help me. You're the only one who knows how. I'll do what you say from now on. Please.

CLARISSE: Well, come with me then, kid. But we got to get out
             of here. It's deep shit city.

They move into the street.

LENA: Johnny was so cold.

CLARISSE: I'll bet. That don't tell you nothing?

LENA: He's probably still mad at me.

CLARISSE: Still mad. Yeah.

LENA: But I love him, Clarisse, more than anything. I don't
             care.

CLARISSE: You're really beautiful, Princess.

LENA: I'm going to find him.

CLARISSE: I bet you will, Princess. I bet you will.

LENA: I'm going to find him soon.

CLARISSE: And I'm going to help you, kid. Yeah, I am. I know a
             lot of Johnnies, you know. One of them's got to be
             yours.

LENA: You're good to me.

CLARISSE: Yeah, I guess I am.

LENA: I want to thank you.

CLARISSE: Let me wear the necklace sometime.

LENA: Johnny gave me this.

CLARISSE: He's got good taste for a Johnny.

LENA: Wear it now.

CLARISSE: You sure?

LENA: Sure thing.

CLARISSE: You're even beautiful without it, Princess. Let's go uptown tonight?

ACT TWO, SCENE TWENTY

A spot reveals BOO and MARTHA.

MARTHA: Boo, make them bring her back. Don't let them take her away.

BOO: Come on, Ma. Come on and sit down.

MARTHA: But they're taking Lena away.

BOO: That's not Lena, Ma.

MARTHA: It's not?

BOO: No, Ma, it's not.

MARTHA: Where is she then?

BOO: I don't know. She ran outside someplace.

MARTHA: The police haven't got her?

BOO: No, they haven't got her.

MARTHA: She can come back then?

BOO: Yeah, she can come back. Why don't you sit down? Somebody's brought you some tea.

MARTHA: She'll come back. She'll apologize.

BOO: Here. Here's my sweater. I'll be right back.

MARTHA: Where you going, Boo?

BOO: I'm going to make a phone call. We need someplace to stay.

MARTHA: Don't you tell that woman what's happened to your sister. Don't let her know.

BOO: Ma, I got to tell her something.

MARTHA: It's none of her business, Daughter.

BOO: Okay, Ma, okay. I won't. I promise I won't.

MARTHA: There's no sugar here, Boo.

BOO: I'll get you some.

MARTHA: She'll come back when she's sorry. She'll apologize to me. *(her spot begins to fade)*

BOO enters a new spot with a pay telephone, puts her coin in and dials, it rings and rings.

BOO: Come on, Aunty. Answer. Answer me. *(she stops the call but just keeps holding on to the receiver)* I need someone to talk to. I need to tell somebody about my shitty day in the big city. There's just some things I can't take care of all by my lonesome. For instance, Aunty, imagine how Coyote cried out when his wife went like a light out of his arms. Can you imagine that? Do you know how long after that Coyote tried to find his way back again to the land of the dead and buried? It was so dumb, Aunty. I mean it was right there under old Coyote's coyote nose. But he couldn't find it again without a spirit guide to save his soul.

Ghosts don't come to those who can't keep their word.

He ended up sitting in an empty place on the plain, pretending under the hot sun to be eating berries and watching horses. He tried to taste the sweetness in his mouth. But when night came down, it was just dust. He never did see that woman of his again in his life. *(she reinserts the coin and dials again; it rings and rings; the spot and the sound begin to fade)*

A spot reveals THOMAS, now a ghost.

THOMAS: Please, I need a drink. I need just one. You got to forgive me. A man could die of thirst around here. I know you think I'm just another drunk Indian. You got to listen to me. Blessed are you among women. I'm in hell, Martha. I'm in hell. You alone can raise me up like a sun. Please, Martha, hear me. Hear my plea. I beg you.

Darkness and the unanswered ringing for four rings. The sound of the receiver hanging up.

THE END

BIG BUCK CITY

A PLAY IN TWO ACTS

Big Buck City was produced at the Tarragon Extra Space from 24 May to 16 June 1991 by Cahoots Theatre Projects with the following cast:

CLARISSE Chrisjohn   Pamela Mathews

BARBARA Buck   Kyra Harper

JACK Buck   Garrison Chrisjohn

RICKY Raccoon   Von Flores

BOO Fisher   Kait Mathews

LENA Fisher   Marion DeVries

Directed by Colin Taylor

Designed by Christine Plunkett

Lighting by Michel Charbonneau

Music by Don Ross

CHARACTERS

CLARISSE Chrisjohn, an Indian woman,
formerly a hooker, now a lay preacher.

BARBARA Buck, an Indian woman, a chatelaine.

JACK Buck, her husband, an Indian business warrior.

BOO Fisher, Barbara's niece through
her older sister Martha.

RICKY Raccoon, an Indian street kid.

LENA Fisher, Barbara's niece,
Boo's older sister, Clarisse's protege
Martha Fisher, see above.

SETTING

The play is set in the living room and the adjacent entry hallway and
front porch of a perfectly renovated house in an old neighbourhood of
the city. A few objects of 'Indianna' decor (*a cigar store Indian, for
instance, might be used as a coat stand*) interrupt the idealized scene, as
do a few Christmas cards and a touch of holiday decoration. The set
is lit like a Christmas tree, lights and darknesses. A large window looks
out to the porch, the street, the night. The front door and the foot of
the up staircase are upstage through a doorway into the hall. The doors
to the kitchen, the basement stairs and the closet are in the same hall
but through an archway downstage.

The action takes place this Christmas eve.

ACT ONE

In the darkness, a turn of jingle bells. Then a green, searching spirit light enters through the window, finds the cuckoo clock and sets it going and then exits into the basement. The basement door slams. Insistent knocking brings up the lights in the street, on the porch. The knocking stops and starts again and stops. The clock cuckoos eight as CLARISSE appears, a silhouette peering in through the front window.

CLARISSE: Holy shit. Hello? Anybody there? Hello? Oh God, they got to be here by now. Oh God.

From upstairs the sound of the toilet flushing. The light in the stairwell comes on.

CLARISSE: Ha! I knew it, I knew it. (*moves back to the door to knock some more*) Hey! Hello up there! Hey, hello! Hey! I got you tidings of great big joy.

The sound off of a car arriving, its door opening and closing.

CLARISSE: Great big joy. Do you hear me? Do you hear the news? Hey, I got the news for you. I know you're up there. Hey, you fuck, I know you're there!

BARBARA: (*enters onto the porch with her arms full of Christmas shopping*) Is there something I can do for you?

CLARISSE: Shit! You scared me, sister.

The sound off of the car departing.

BARBARA: So is there something you want here?

116

CLARISSE: I've got some great news for you.

BARBARA: Look, my dear, I really don't have time right now. Christmas Eve and all, and as you can see, I've already spent all my money.

CLARISSE: Nah, that's not it, lady.

BARBARA: I really have nothing left. I had to give the cab driver all my change.

CLARISSE: You Martha Fisher? Martha Fisher?

BARBARA: No, I'm not.

CLARISSE: She lives here, don't she?

BARBARA: Look, Martha doesn't have any money either.

CLARISSE: You her sister? This here's the right address?

BARBARA: Now what sort of business could you have with Martha?

CLARISSE: Oh, lady, I bring her tidings of great joy. Let me talk to her.

BARBARA: Look, my dear, you can talk to me.

CLARISSE: This message is for her.

BARBARA: You can tell me.

CLARISSE: Time is of the essence, lady.

BARBARA: I know what time it is. *(finds her key and opens the door)*

CLARISSE: Look, tell her it's about the Princess, okay?

BARBARA: Why can't you come back at some more opportune time? It's not like it's the end of the world.

CLARISSE: Lady, something big is happening.

BARBARA: Please. Martha cannot see you. Martha isn't feeling well.

CLARISSE: Well, this will make her feel better. I guarantee glad tidings.

BARBARA: Well, we've had enough of your glad tidings! For Christ sake, it's Christmas! Can't you people give us a break?. Leave us alone. Peace on earth!

The clock starts cuckooing.

BARBARA: Stop harassing us. Just because we're Indians.

CLARISSE: Shit, what time's that?

BARBARA: You can't barge in here and expect handouts. We worked hard to get where we are.

CLARISSE: Look, lady, I got to go—

BARBARA: You can't take advantage of us!

CLARISSE: —I got to go! But I'll be back, I'll be back!

BARBARA: I'll call the police!

CLARISSE: I promise you you shall behold the Handmaid of the
             Lord! *(hurries off down the street)* The Handmaid of
             the Lord!

BARBARA: I'll call the police! Stay away! You stay away or I'll call
             the police. *(she enters the house, slamming the door,
             dropping her shopping onto the couch in the living
             room; she slaps the cuckoo clock into silence, then turns
             a lamp on and hangs her coat on the stand in the hall-
             way)* Martha! Martha, hon, are you awake?

*The toilet flushes. BARBARA turns on the tape deck to play a back-
ground of Christmas music before picking up the mail inside the front
door and sitting down in the chair to read.*

*She is pleased by the pair of Christmas cards and places them prettily on
the coffee table. She is troubled by what appears to be a business letter
and forces herself to read it a second time.*

*The sound off of a car arriving. A moment later JACK enters through the
front door.*

JACK: Hiya, Babsy. *(throws his coat on the couch)* How's my
             Pocahontas tonight? What do you say?

BARBARA: I'm okay.

JACK: 'Okay?' Where's your Christmas spirit, babe? Do I
             have to get out the mistletoe?

BARBARA: No, Jack.

JACK: A guy likes a little more warmth, Babsy. It's a cold world out there. Leave me pour you a drink. *(he stops by the empty telephone table)* Hey,, Babsy! The telephone?

BARBARA: I just got home myself. *(she drops the letter into one of her shopping bags)*

JACK: Your sister's got shit for brains, Babsy. Where was it the last time?

BARBARA: The closet.

JACK: I thought we'd worked this out. *(sits his brief case down)* How many times I got to explain it to her? Can't she understand? Babsy, how we supposed to live if I can't do business? I got to get the news.

BARBARA: Jack, if we could just put it away when we go out—

JACK: I ain't got time for this shit, Babsy. We're down to our last pitiful phone on account of her nerves! She's got to learn to behave.

BARBARA: She just hates telephones, Jack.

JACK: I love telephones, Babsy. I hear that little ring-a-ding and I'm alive. The hunt is on.

BARBARA: She's my sister, Jack.

JACK: Don't tell me it runs in the family, babe.

BARBARA: You know she's worried. You know she's scared.

JACK: We lost that gorgeous house over in the west end on account of her. Now that's scary. *(he opens the closet)*

BARBARA: I know you think it's silly.

JACK: Phone calls from the dead? Shit, I said 'scary.' Real scary.

BARBARA: She's superstitious, Jack. She just doesn't understand city life.

JACK: Maybe she'd understand room and board. *(he searches the closet)*

BARBARA: Jack, how can you say that?

JACK: Aha! *(brings the telephone out)* Pay dirt!

BARBARA: How can you say that and talk about the Christmas spirit?

JACK: That's better. Here's our line to what matters.

BARBARA: She doesn't mean to be a problem.

JACK: She showed up here, didn't she?

BARBARA: She's my sister, Jack. We have to take care of her. People will take advantage if we don't.

JACK: Shit draws flies, Babsy.

BARBARA: They took all her money!

JACK: Rolled by the holy rollers.

BARBARA: She didn't know any better. You could trust people
              where we grew up.

JACK: In the fucking bush. She should have come here first.

BARBARA: Boo said she was afraid to let us know what hap-
              pened.

JACK: Can you blame her? I wish you hadn't told me. Who
              needs to know this crap?

BARBARA: She really believes it, Jack.

JACK: A killer ghost named Johnny is after her little Lena.
              That is a scary pile of it.

BARBARA: That's why Lena came to the city. Johnny called her
              on the telephone.

JACK: Listen to yourself. Do you hear what you're saying?

BARBARA: It's what Martha believes.

JACK: You believe it too, don't you? My Babs is still a bush
              Indian.

BARBARA: No, I don't, Jack.

JACK: You'd be off with them holy rollers too, if it weren't for
              me.

BARBARA: No, Jack. I know what they are now. One of them was
              on the porch when I got home. One of them holy
              rollers.

JACK:	Was he at least entertaining?
BARBARA:	It was a woman. An Indian woman. She knew Martha's name.
JACK:	The shit heads won't even let us keep our souls.
BARBARA:	She wanted to tell Martha about Christmas.
JACK:	I'd like to tell her something too. But we'd have to get her her own phone for Christmas just to get through.
BARBARA:	That's silly, Jack.
JACK:	And a spot in the basement for her to bury it in. Shit, if I'd known she was going to stay this long, I'd have at least got another line installed down there in the dungeon. *(he plugs the telephone in)*
BARBARA:	I'm sorry it's not a good place for an office.
JACK:	'Not good', babe! It's embarrassing. I'm not supposed to be doing business in toilets.
BARBARA:	Well, we couldn't ask her to sleep down there.
JACK:	I think I could. If I ever saw Madame Fisher.
BARBARA:	I think she doesn't want to come down and upset you.
JACK:	Upset me? Upset me! Babe, she hasn't been down those stairs in three days. Or out of the house in – how long?
BARBARA:	The traffic scares her.

JACK: Everything scares her. Shit. If we could just get her to
               a shrink.

BARBARA: She's not crazy, Jack. She's just upset.

JACK: Let's get this straight. Your dear old sis, Martha the
               Fisher, is afraid her streetwalking daughter—

BARBARA: Lena's not a streetwalker.

JACK: —has been killed by a ghost, and is going to call her
               collect.

BARBARA: Jack, it's not funny.

JACK: And you're telling me the woman who believes this
               crapola is just upset! Babe, we're living our lives like
               it's Hallowe'en. It's supposed to be fucking Christmas.

BARBARA: How would you feel if your child ran away like that?

RICKY appears at the window, casing the joint and its occupants.

BARBARA: Think about it, Jack. She's had a rotten life.

JACK: Okay, okay, Babsy. So old Martha's had a rotten life.
               And she's sharing the stink with us. But (*opens his
               brief case and produces a bottle of good scotch*) looky
               what I got here. How's this for the sweet life? How's
               this for the Christmas spirit in the flesh? This'll put a
               star in your eyes. I gave myself a bonus on that condo
               I closed on last week. This might make old Martha
               feel better. Invite the cold Fish down for a drink.

BARBARA: Don't call her that, Jack.

JACK: And how could I forget! She won't drink either. The
               good Christian and her rotten life. Real rotten.

The telephone rings.

JACK: Get the glasses, Babsy. *(turns the tape deck off)* We'll
               have us a drink, okay? Just us two for a change.
               (answers the phone) Hello? Ya, you got him, chief.

BARBARA: Jack. Jack!

JACK: *(on the phone)* Just a sec. *(to BARBARA)* What is it?

BARBARA: Don't talk too long. Please. It is Christmas eve.

JACK: Sure thing. And we got them reservations, right?

BARBARA: Like all good Indians.

JACK: That's my Babsy. Get them glasses. *(on the phone)*
               Okay. So what's the big deal?

BARBARA takes the bottle off into the kitchen. RICKY disappears.

JACK: Ya. So what? Okay, that makes sense. Okey-dokey.
               Oh, now we're talking green stuff. You're sure about
               this now? Ya, I know, but I love the look of the place.
               And none of them yuppies are going to look into the
               plumbing. We fumigate it and all we got to do is go in
               for the kill. It'll be mouth-watering.

*BARBARA returns with the bottle, glasses and ice on a tray. She pours
the drinks and clears the packages off the couch.*

JACK: So how much do you think? That all? Holy Christ, he
             must be getting old. Ya, I know, you got to keep up
             with the pack. So what's the profit margin on that?
             Come on. Let's get this straight. Really? You get new
             batteries for Christmas. Ya, I promise.

*BARBARA starts to unpack her shopping but when she comes to the letter,
she stops and drops it back into the bag. She gets her drink and, leaving
JACK his, goes to stare out the window into the night.*

JACK: I ain't got all night, man. All right! Gimme five – hun-
             dred thousand! Hell, if we can pull this off, we're
             smiling dollars. We're in heaven. We'll be pissing with
             the big guys. Ya, no kidding. Look, I got to go. Christ-
             mas Eve chow down. Ya, ciao. *(he hangs up)* Hey, Babsy,
             thanks for the drink. What you looking at?

BARBARA: It looks cold out there. Do you think it will snow?

JACK: Dammit, Babsy, you're glum again. 'Tis the season to
             be jolly.

BARBARA: That's just it, Jack. I want it to be a white Christmas.

JACK: Hey, that'd be great, wouldn't it? Like a Christmas
             card.

BARBARA: There were a couple more today. The one from the dry
             cleaners is pretty.

JACK: Ya? I bet the buggers are trying to make up for that
             shirt they lost.

BARBARA: Jack, have we had a frost this year?

JACK: It's pretty warm out there, Babsy. Sort of like you.

BARBARA: Not now, Jack.

JACK: Come on, Babsy. Come to your Big Buck.

BARBARA: Boo will be back any minute.

JACK: She can go fuck herself.

BARBARA: Jack, no. We have to get going soon.

JACK: We do, do we? Too late for another drink?

BARBARA: Not for me.

JACK: Hey, I don't see what's wrong with green for Christ-
               mas. Green looks pretty good to me, if you know what
               I mean. Hey, looky here what I got for my Babsy. *(he
               produces a jewellery box from this pocket)*

BARBARA: *(opens the box and removes a gold necklace)* Oh Jack,
               it's gorgeous.

JACK: Sorry I didn't get around to wrapping it up. It's sup-
               posed to be handmade.

BARBARA: I can tell. It's got a sort of glow.

JACK: I figured you'd like it.

BARBARA: We should have waited at least until midnight.

JACK: It's too late now, Babsy. Santa's off schedule.

BARBARA: This is the Christmas spirit, Jack, this glow.

JACK: Talk about a pretty penny, Babsy. Why don't you wear it tonight?

BARBARA: Will it go with my dress?

JACK: Better than all that turquoise shit.

BARBARA: I like my turquoise, Jack.

RICKY appears again at the window.

BARBARA: Why don't I just wrap it up so Boo and Martha can see?

JACK: You know how crazy you are?

BARBARA: I think Martha would like it too.

JACK: Ya. Well, I would like another drink. How about you?

BARBARA: Oh Jack!

JACK: What is it?

BARBARA: Can I give it to Martha?

JACK: What? Do what you want, Babsy.

BARBARA: *(puts the box beside the Christmas cards)* You didn't get her anything, did you, Jack?

JACK: Me? How about a bus ticket back to the bush?

BARBARA: It's all right, Jack. I got her something. It can be from both of us. Do you want to know what it is?

JACK: Surprise me.

RICKY disappears.

BARBARA: You don't care about snow, do you?

JACK: We got lots of ice. What more do you need?

BARBARA: Why won't it snow here, Jack? What's wrong with the world?

JACK: Nothing's wrong with the world. It's just the greenhouse effect. Money, Babsy, lots of money.

The clock starts cuckooing. JACK salutes it with his drink and it falls silent.

BARBARA: *(turns the Christmas tape back on)* It doesn't seem like Christmas.

JACK: Look, Babsy, Santa Claus will come tonight and make everything all right.

BARBARA: All I really want is snow.

JACK: Okay, okay, whatever you say. I'll phone Joe and see if I can still get an order in.

BARBARA: Joe? Joe who?

JACK: Joe the Weatherman. You want it all dressed? All the trimmings? They should have snowflakes, snow banks. What do you say? They might even have icicles.

BARBARA: Okay. Snowflakes, icicles, everything. After all, it is Christmas.

JACK starts to dial.

BARBARA: Jack. Jack, who're you calling?

JACK: The weatherman, Babsy.

BARBARA: Jack, please, no more business stuff today.

JACK: Just one more call, Babs. I just remembered something.

BARBARA: Jack, please, take a holiday. You promised you'd take a holiday. You promised me we'd celebrate.

JACK: Okay. *(he hangs up)* So I made the reservations. For four, God help me. Are you ready? Is the cold Fish? I'm all set and raring to celebrate.

BARBARA: She will be. I told her this morning. I'll go check right now. We can go soon as Boo gets in.

JACK picks up his briefcase.

BARBARA: Where you going?

JACK: Just to put this on my desk.

BARBARA: Jack, if you go down there, you'll start doing something. I won't be able to get you up here again tonight.

JACK: Come on, Babsy, you're always after me to put my shit
               away.

BARBARA: Well, tonight you're on holiday. (*she takes the briefcase
               away from him and puts it in the closet*)

JACK: So what do I do while I wait?

BARBARA: Have another drink.

JACK: You trying to get me drunk, babe? It'll be your own
               fault.

BARBARA: I'll go check on Martha.

JACK: She like Italian?

BARBARA: I don't think she's even heard of Italian.

JACK: Just tell her it's the original Kraft dinner.

BARBARA: She really hasn't been out all week.

JACK: She'll enjoy this then. You want – what is it, babe?

BARBARA: I got this letter today.

JACK: The report from the bank? About time. They prom-
               ised it would be here weeks ago.

The telephone starts ringing.

BARBARA: Jack, please don't answer that.

JACK: It's probably Joe. The guy who makes the wind?

BARBARA:	I need to talk to you.
JACK:	It'll just be a second. (*answers the phone*) Hello. Oh hiya. Well 'How' to you too.
BARBARA:	Hang it up, Jack.
JACK:	(*to BARBARA*) Just a sec, Babs. It's the Loan Arranger. (*on the phone*) So what's cooking, kemo sabe?
BARBARA:	You owe me, Jack. I said 'You owe me!' (*grabs the receiver*)
JACK:	Hey, Babsy, what is this?
BARBARA:	(*on the phone*) Jack can't talk to you right now. He has some personal business to deal with. No, no, I'm sorry. Call back after Christmas. (*she hangs up*)
JACK:	Babsy, what the fuck is this all about?
BARBARA:	You're taking a holiday from that stuff.

The telephone starts ringing again. BARBARA unplugs it and puts it away back in the closet.

JACK:	Babsy, it could be that mortgage.
BARBARA:	The banks are all closed, aren't they?
JACK:	Shit, you're getting as potty as your sister.
BARBARA:	I just want to talk to you about this letter.
JACK:	So? So what is it?

BARBARA: It's from the clinic.

JACK: I sent them jerks a cheque last week.

BARBARA: No, Jack, not a bill.

JACK: I should hope not. So what is it? What did old Doctor Bones have to say for himself? Was he asking for another donation? He'll squeeze us dry.

BARBARA: Jack, a personal letter. To both of us.

JACK: So what's the deal, Babsy?

BARBARA: You might be glad to know he doesn't think we should waste any more money on his treatment.

JACK: Let me see that thing. That old quack. That fucking quack. He can't do this to us. He's bled us for too much already. He signed a contract.

BARBARA: Jack, it's over now.

JACK: Look, Babsy, we'll find somebody else. Get a second opinion, shop around. We're going to take out our options, Babsy.

BARBARA: Jack, he knows what he's talking about. He's the best in the field. He's just being honest with us.

JACK: Honest? Fuck honest. It's too late for honest. I never trusted the guy. What kind of man makes a living looking up women's skirts? Shit, we'll get that operation.

BARBARA: I'm too old, Jack.

JACK: We'll get that operation and we won't let him do it. We'll take our business elsewhere.

BARBARA: Jack, that's just being childish.

JACK: Lots of women your age have kids. You're not that old.

BARBARA: Not for the first time, Jack.

JACK: I knew them stupid pills wouldn't work. Hormones, my ass.

BARBARA: Jack, please, I just don't want to talk about it anymore.

JACK: You got to do more than that when the plumbing's screwed up.

BARBARA: Jack, I don't want to yell anymore.

JACK: We're not quitting. We can afford the best. I'm going to get on it right away.

BARBARA: No, Jack, no. I don't want to try anymore. I want to give up.

JACK: Hey, Babsy, us Bucks don't give up. Us Bucks are winners. Us Bucks are going to have a son.

BARBARA: Jack, please, I'm tired. I'm tired of all of it. I hate that place. I hate the tests. It makes me feel so dirty. I'm tired of all those white men. I don't want them touching me.

JACK: Come on, Babsy, get a hold on it. Come on, babe. We
               don't talk about it no more.

BARBARA: I wanted this to be a good Christmas.

JACK: Come on. I'm here. Big Buck's here. We're together,
               babe.

BOO peeks in the window, taps on the glass and waves.

JACK: Look who's back. Scared it right out of you, didn't
               she? Shit, Babsy, you're always telling her to knock.

*BOO knocks. JACK opens the front door for her. BOO drags in a scrag-
gly Christmas tree.*

BOO: Hey, I got you guys a fertility symbol!

JACK: Why can't you remember your key?

BOO: Not that you look like you need it.

BARBARA: We were just talking.

JACK: It's kind of pitiful looking.

BOO: It's the best they had left. But it's the thought, right,
               Auntie?

BARBARA: We were just talking.

BOO: It looked like a pretty intense conversation. Auntie, I
               think you're blushing.

BARBARA: I wish you wouldn't talk like that.

BOO: Come on, Auntie, I'm not a kid.

JACK: Ya, Babsy, she didn't mean any harm. She was just joking around.

BARBARA: It's not funny, Jack.

JACK: Babsy, where are you going?

BARBARA: I've got to change this dress and put my face on if we're going out to dinner.

BOO: Careful, Auntie. Sometimes the way you wear that stuff so thick it looks like Uncle's been slapping you around.

BARBARA: Who told you that? Who said that?

BOO: Nobody, Auntie. Nobody. Honest.

BARBARA: Do you sit around thinking up these things you say?

BOO: Auntie, this is the way I talk.

BARBARA: They just come out that way! This is a nice neighbourhood. This isn't the bush. You can't go around just shooting off your mouth.

BOO: I guess I'm just a wild Indian.

BARBARA: Boo, not everyone has your sense of humour, you know. What if someone heard you say that? What would they think?

JACK: Try to be civilized, kiddo.

BOO: I'm sorry. I didn't mean nothing, Auntie.

BARBARA: Nothing. That's what it will get us. Don't you ever talk
                that way in front of your mother.

BOO: My Ma doesn't give a sh— she wouldn't notice, Auntie.
                I'm sorry.

The clock starts cuckooing. BARBARA slaps it silent.

JACK: Careful with that, Babsy. Please.

BARBARA: I'll see if Martha's ready. *(she exits upstairs)*

BOO: Her Christmas spirit evaporated kind of fast.

JACK: This really is kind of pitiful.

BOO: It must be because it's so hot in here.

JACK: Hey, college girl, put a lid on that shitty talk when
                your aunt's around.

BOO: What's pissed you off?

JACK: Nothing. It's just Christmas.

BOO: Somebody tell you the truth about Santa Claus?

JACK: Your aunt's worried about your mother. You know? The
                mother who hasn't been downstairs all week. What do
                you think about that? Didn't you know?

BOO: I been busy.

JACK: There's more to life than Christmas shopping, kid.

BOO: That would be news in this house.

JACK: Look, you can't expect your aunt to be your mother's keeper. You got to pay your share. Well?

BOO: I got a new lead.

JACK: How many times have I heard that one before? Have you told your mother? Why not? It might get her off her duff.

BOO: I don't want to disappoint her.

JACK: Kid, your big sister's out there walking the streets. How could you be a disappointment?

BOO: You don't know if that's true.

JACK: She walked off with a hooker. Use your head, little girl. Your sis is in the business by now for sure.

BOO: Ma doesn't need to know that stuff.

JACK: Your mother needs to get real. So do you, Booster. Seems her old mental bank account has a few cents missing.

BOO: Uncle, she can't handle all that shit.

JACK: Your mother needs a head doctor, kid.

BOO: She's just confused.

JACK: Phone calls from the dead is just confused?

BOO: I heard it ring too, Uncle.

JACK: You never heard of a party line?

BOO: Look, Uncle. Look. I saw Johnny too. I saw the ghost. In the bar.

JACK: What gets into you women!

BOO: I even talked to him.

JACK: You poor kid! It does run in the family.

BOO: There's nothing wrong with me.

JACK: How come you never told me before, Booster?

BOO: I didn't want to upset you.

JACK: But I don't get upset! See, Boo? I'm sorry for you.

BOO: There's nothing wrong with me, Uncle.

JACK: And we've been letting you wander around out there. No wonder you can't find your sister. You're not even in the same city, are you?

BOO: I knew I shouldn't have told you.

JACK: And here I thought all this sweetgrass stink was for your mother's sake. I need a drink.

BOO: Uncle, I got a lead.

RICKY is at the window again.

JACK: Sure you do, Booster.

BOO: I do, Uncle.

JACK: Where did all that money go? Up in smoke? Tell me it's not drugs.

BOO: This Indian kid I met saw her.

JACK: Are you sure he's not a ghost too, Boo?

RICKY disappears.

BOO: He's seen her, Uncle.

JACK: They've all seen her.

BOO: No, I didn't offer no money or nothing like that this time. I just told him about Lena and that woman and he said he thought he'd seen her on a streetcar.

JACK: Just like that?

BOO: I been hanging around with him. About a month now. To get him to trust me.

JACK: To get him to trust you! You don't know who he is.

BOO: He's from up north. His name's Ricky. Ricky Raccoon.

JACK: You're kidding. This is just great. A fucking bush Indian named Ricky Raccoon. Has he got you buying him beer?

BOO: He's not old enough. We have coffee. And he likes hot
            chocolate.

JACK: Hot chocolate! So how much does he owe you?

BOO: He's got money himself. He even treats me some-
            times. I'm getting real close.

JACK: To who? What you been doing for a month? Dating?
            Has he put the moves on you, Boo?

BOO: It's not like that. I told you. He's just a kid.

JACK: Cradle-robbing just to get a date! And I thought your
            mother was potty.

BOO: I said 'It's not like that.'

JACK: And your sister's naughty! Oh this is nice.

BOO: Uncle, how much have you had?

JACK: Not enough. Too much. No wonder we lost the coun-
            try. We're a bunch of fucking idiots.

The toilet flushes.

BOO: Uncle, why don't you sit down?

JACK: I need more ice.

BOO: Uncle! Uncle, he mentioned her necklace.

JACK: What necklace?

BOO: The gold chain that Johnny gave her.

JACK: A gold chain. I guess no ghost would be interested in that.

BOO: He mentioned it first. But it's pretty. Anybody would notice.

JACK: 'It's got a sort of glow.' Shit.

BOO: He's going to find out where they live.

JACK: You shouldn't be doing this, Booster. They always take you.

BOO: I'm going to meet him day after tomorrow. He ain't got a phone. And he doesn't know I'm staying here.

JACK: So?

BOO: Look, Uncle Jack. I could have Ma back home in the bush with Lena by New Year's. You could get your office back.

JACK: Shit, I can't tell if these tidings are glad or mad.

BOO: You've had too much to drink, Uncle.

JACK: Hell, tell the old Fish. For Christ sake, it's Christmas. We might as well have something to celebrate, I guess.

BOO: I'll see how Ma's feeling.

JACK: Tell your mother. You want me to do it?

BOO: I guess it wouldn't hurt.

JACK: How about right now? Come on, Booster. Do it for Uncle Buck. Then we can all have a drink.

BOO: Oh, all right. *(she exits upstairs)*

JACK: And put on something decent. This restaurant's a nice place. Fuck, I can't believe this. I'm living in a house full of *(realizes the ice is all gone)* – shit. Women! *(exits to the kitchen)*

RICKY *reappears at the window.*

JACK: *(enters with the ice, pours a drink, looks at his watch, wanders over to nudge the tree with a toe)* Pitiful thing. *(puts down his glass and exits into the basement)*

RICKY *disappears.*

BARBARA: *(entering downstairs)* Jack. Jack? *(looks in kitchen)* Jack, where are you? *(looks down into the basement)* Jack, you're not down there! Oh Jack, you promised. I said 'You promised.'

JACK: *(entering from the basement with a large box)* I'm just going to set up that tree, Babsy. You going to let me by?

BARBARA: Sorry.

JACK: I'm going to decorate us Bucks a bush the whole block will envy, Babsy.

BARBARA: That's nice, Jack, but she won't get up.

JACK: *(finds the Christmas tree stand)* Then we'll see about
                 the Christmas spirit.

BARBARA: Jack, Martha won't get up.

JACK: Ho ho ho, if you know what I mean. *(places the Christ-
                 mas tree stand)* How's that?

BARBARA: Jack, we can't go out.

JACK: Is the Boo talking to her?

BARBARA: Yes, but she doesn't want to come. She said she heard
                 noises on the roof.

JACK: Tell her it's too early for Rudolph. Hey, look at this,
                 Santa's beard. And here's the hat.

BARBARA: She's not even dressed.

JACK: *(puts the hat and beard on)* How do I look? I could go
                 like this.

BARBARA: Don't you dare. People already think you dress funny.

JACK: I like to get them while they're laughing. Hey. Who's
                 Big Chief of the Tipis in the Big Smoke?

BARBARA: You are.

JACK: I think this'll do the job. Is it Christmas Eve or what?
                 Here, let me get you some of the spirit.

BARBARA: No, Jack, you've had too much yourself.

JACK: At least try to have some fun, babe.

BARBARA: I just want an aperitif at the restaurant.

JACK: Look. You said the Boo's talking to her, right? Well, there's news. Some kid's seen Lena. I think it's for real this time. If that doesn't perk old Martha up, she can just go fuck herself.

BARBARA: Jack!

JACK: (*plunking the tree into the stand*) We're going to have a merry old time tonight. We deserve it.

BARBARA: You're not being fair.

JACK: I'm not being fair? You know what the Boo told me? Do you? She told me she saw that ghost too!

BARBARA: She promised not to tell you.

JACK: You knew? You knew we had two shitheads on our hands and you didn't tell me?

BARBARA: I didn't want you to get upset.

JACK: Everybody's so nice to me!

BARBARA: You said you didn't want to hear it.

JACK: Let's get this straight. The old Fisher and her daughter show up out of nowhere after how many years of silence like your family was dead? How many? And we put them up out of the goodness of our hearts and pocket books and put up with her whining—

BARBARA: She lost her baby.

JACK: —her whining about her delinquent daughter, her pretty little Lena, for the worst part of a year. We decide Oh, we can't go to Mexico – we have to be here for her. And we decide Oh we can't go dancing – we have to be here for her. And I can't invite the guys over for meetings because it might upset Martha to see all those pale faces to say nothing of the fact that old cold Fisher face depresses the shit out of everyone from the real world. And now I discover the Boo is spooky too and Princess, you say you don't want me to get upset!

The toilet flushes.

JACK: What is wrong with that woman?

BARBARA: I just wanted us all to be together tonight. Like a family.

JACK: I say okay if she comes. But I say we go without her if we have to. There ain't that many good places open for business on Christmas Eve, Babsy. But we got an in at the inn!

BARBARA: She must be getting dressed by now.

JACK: We're having a good time. Ho ho ho!

BARBARA: There's your pillow there, Jack. Here. Saint Nick always has a tummy.

JACK: *(poses with the pillow)* Ho ho ho—like a bowl full of jelly!

BARBARA: *(helps him reach the straps)* Hold still, you silly. Oh Jack.

JACK: What is it?

BARBARA: You look like you're due any minute.

JACK: Don't cry on me, babe. *(throws the pillow aside)* It is Christmas. You want to help me finish setting up that tree?

BARBARA: Maybe we could all decorate it together after we get back? With popcorn.

JACK: That's my corn princess! And Santa can come down the drainpipe and give out our presents at midnight.

BARBARA: And we can open them all together. Jack?

JACK: What is it, babe?

BARBARA: I want to go to church. To the midnight service.

JACK: You'll miss Mister Claus when he comes.

BARBARA: You don't have to come with me if you don't want. I bet Martha would like to go with me.

JACK: I bet she would.

BARBARA: I like the carols, Jack. I'm sorry.

JACK: You're just a little bush Indian at heart. Like the rest of them. Superstitious as shit. Tra-la-la-la-la.

BARBARA: I'm sorry, Jack. I try.

JACK: I know you do, Bush Baby. I'm just teasing.

BARBARA: We're going to be late, aren't we? We'll be right back down. *(exits upstairs)*

JACK: *(takes off the beard and sips his drink; examines a branch of the tree)* You're kind of dry, aren't you? Here, let me get you a drink. *(throws the ice water into the stand's bucket)* Hey, don't mind if I do. *(freshens his own drink, then pours some whiskey into the bucket)* That's just between me and you, you know. Joy of the season. Hey, you'll really be lit up! Don't mind if I do. *(pours himself another shot; the clock cuckoos once)* You're telling me. *(bolts the drink, then digs the rest of the Santa suit – pants, jacket, boots and belt – out of the box and lays it out on the couch; digs out some miscellaneous decorations and puts them on the tree)* Where's your fucking star? *(finds a string of lights and awkwardly arranges it on the tree; plugs it in; nothing)* Father fucking Christmas. *(kicks at the plug and the lights begin flashing)* Hey, what did I tell you? *(pours himself another shot)* To the ghost of Christmas presents!

BOO and BARBARA enter downstairs.

BOO: I don't think so.

BARBARA: But she said to, Boo.

BOO: She doesn't mean it.

BARBARA: Your mother just needs time to herself.

BOO: But she's been alone all day.

JACK: What the fuck is it now?

BOO: She was going to come.

The toilet flushes.

BOO: I shouldn't have told her about Ricky. She got weird
            about it and locked herself in the bathroom.

BARBARA: She's just upset, Boo.

BOO: She asked me if I thought I was on holiday.

BARBARA: You'll find Lena. Your mother knows that in her heart.
            We all know you'll find your sister.

JACK: We're praying you do.

BARBARA: Jack, could you just go up and talk to Martha?

JACK: No fucking way.

BARBARA: How much have you had to drink?

BOO: Auntie came up and suddenly Ma went all white.

BARBARA: I just thought she should think about the rest of us for
            a change.

BOO: Now she won't come out. I think I better stay home.

JACK: Come on, kid. No reason for her to poop our party.

BOO: You and Uncle Jack go by yourselves.

BARBARA: No. If anybody stays here with your mother, I will. I'm
            her sister. But I won't. She can't go on like this.
            Christmas is a family occasion and if your mother
            chooses to forget it, it's her decision.

BOO: It's not like we're all here, Auntie.

JACK: You can say that again.

BARBARA: Well, we're going to make do.

JACK: Kid, as a favour to me, the guy who buys the tele-
            phones. Your aunt wants to see you have a good time.

BOO: I don't know. I'd be thinking about Ma.

BARBARA: Well, you know very well she's not thinking about you.
            Has she once thought about you, Boo?

BOO: But I can take care of myself.

BARBARA: Lena was her first-born, Boo.

JACK: Come on. We're late. (*giving BARBARA her coat*) We
            could lose our place and they'll charge me for the
            reservations anyway.

BARBARA: Boo, listen. Fettucine Alfredo.

BOO: Well, I guess I am hungry.

BARBARA: We'll come right back.

JACK: Come on, come on. (*getting his coat*)

BARBARA: Here are the keys.

JACK: I'll drive.

BARBARA: No, you won't. Leave the glass.

JACK: Well, let's hurry. I got a penny to spend and I can't do
              it here, thanks to dear Martha.

BOO: Here. I'll drive.

*They exit out front, BOO last, turning off the tape deck, the hall light
and the living room lamp.*

*The tree is blinking. The sound of the car starting up and driving off.
Glass breaking in the basement, then something falling over. The blinking hesitates. The toilet flushes.*

*RICKY enters from the basement, a screwdriver in hand. The blinking
continues. RICKY checks out the tape deck's connections, then surveys
the room. He opens JACK's bottle of scotch and takes a swig and spits it
out. RICKY finds the jewellery box, looks inside and then pockets it. The
clock cuckoos once and RICKY checks it out too. He notices the blinking tree. When he takes in the intoxicating aroma, he stumbles and tum-
bles backward into the box of decorations. He comes up with a wreath
around his neck. He finds a small model manger which he places prettily
under the tree with the scotch bottle in it. He puts a few decorations on
the tree and arranges the packages under it.*

*Then he notices the Santa suit. He checks the pants and jacket out for
size against his legs and arms and then discards the wreath. He takes off
his denim jacket and puts the Santa jacket on over his Indian T-shirt. He
takes off his raccoon hat and puts on the beard and Santa hat. He checks*

out his reflection in the window and does a silent little Fancy Dance. The sound off of a car arriving. He drops to the floor and pulls off his sneakers and jeans. He stands up and reaches for the Santa pants. He hesitates, realizing the audience sees his partial nakedness, and wags a finger at them. Insistent knocking at the door. CLARISSE is on the porch. RICKY grabs the pants and boots and ducks out of sight behind the couch as CLARISSE comes to peer in the window.

CLARISSE: Hey. Hello in there. Hey! Anybody there? Shit. *(she knocks again at the door)* Hey, I know you're in there, lady. Hey. Come on. Come on out. I got big news. Great big news for your house. Hey, you fuck, hurry up!

RICKY has finished putting the Santa suit on, including pants, boots, and belly pillow, and now goes into the hallway to turn the light on and open the door a crack.

CLARISSE: Hiya. Sorry I took so long. I got to talk to the Fisher lady now. You know? Martha. Like immediately. I got tidings of great big joy to her.

RICKY: *(opening the door all the way)* Ho ho ho!

CLARISSE: Oh, hiya Santa. Out early tonight, ain't you? What you doing here?

RICKY bows for her to enter.

CLARISSE: Thanks a lot. You're a doll. So can I see that lady Martha now? Like now?

RICKY turns the lamp on and motions for CLARISSE to sit.

CLARISSE: What? I don't want to. Sit yourself. Wait a sec. You going to get her? Okay, but I'm in a hurry.

RICKY heads for the staircase.

CLARISSE: Time is of the essence, Nick. I got a surprise out in the cab.

RICKY changes direction and heads out the front door and off toward the cab.

CLARISSE: *(follows him out as far as the porch)* Hey, wait a sec. Santa! Santa. Hey, you fuck, come back here. Oh shit, what do you think you're doing? Lena! Lena, stay put! Go back! Jesus, Princess, we don't got time to visit here. What did you get out for?

LENA: *(most pregnant, enters onto the porch)* I had a pain. It's not so bad when I move around.

CLARISSE: You okay?

LENA: *(peers in the open door)* Where are we, Clarisse?

CLARISSE: The address your Momma left at the mission, Princess. You should have stayed put.

LENA: Santa sent me in.

The sound off of a car departing hurriedly.

CLARISSE: Oh shit, what's with that cabby?

LENA: I bet he's running away. Santa tried to kiss him on the lips.

CLARISSE: But he can't take off and leave us.

LENA: I think I scared him too. I made a lot of noise.

CLARISSE: I was counting on him. Cabbies are supposed to know what to do.

LENA: *(steps inside)* Oh, Clarisse, look. A tree.

A light on the Christmas tree burns out.

CLARISSE: Maybe somebody here can drive us.

RICKY enters, shooing CLARISSE inside, shutting the door.

CLARISSE: Don't touch me, you.

LENA: Isn't it nice, Clarisse?

CLARISSE: Bug off, Santa. We don't need this crap, Lena. Leave that thing alone.

LENA: Makes me think of home. It's nice out there now.

CLARISSE: Too cold for this urbane Indian.

LENA: Lots of snow. What is it, Santa? What does he mean?

CLARISSE: I don't know. God, I hate mime. Look, Santa, where's the old lady? Is she still here or not? Wait a sec already.

RICKY exits to the kitchen.

CLARISSE: Shit. Hello! Hello? Hey, I got big news! I'll go check out the place, Princess. You take the load off while you can.

LENA: I'm fine now, Clarisse.

CLARISSE: You sure? What about the pains? You got to pamper yourself, Princess.

LENA: Who you looking for, Clarisse?

CLARISSE: Your momma and your sister.

LENA: Here. Boo's here?

CLARISSE: Pay attention to me. You ought to sit down.

LENA: How would she get here?

CLARISSE: You're the Handmaid of the Lord, Lena. This is a miracle you're about to do.

LENA: What would Boo be doing in a place like this?

CLARISSE: It ain't exactly hot shit, I admit. Come back here, Princess.

LENA: Clarisse, Boo's not here.

CLARISSE: Look, Princess, park it. Let me go look for her.

LENA: Don't go, Clarisse.

CLARISSE: Let me do my duty. Prepare ye the way of the Lord. Make His paths straight.

LENA: It's no use. She's not here.

CLARISSE: It's a new world coming, kid. And you're the one cho-
             sen to deliver it in one pretty little package.

LENA: Oh, maybe I should sit down.

CLARISSE: I want you to be okay.

LENA: I'm fine. Don't fuss.

CLARISSE: Hope was growing inside you when I met you, Prin-
             cess. What a glow you had. What I didn't know!

LENA: You're just an old auntie, Clarisse.

CLARISSE: Here I thought it was some nothing lover man. But
             this is a most holy and mysterious event.

LENA: Don't talk about it, Clarisse.

CLARISSE: You saved my life, Princess.

LENA: All that stuff with Johnny's over with now.

CLARISSE: I want to do this right.

LENA: I think I need the ladies' again, Clarisse.

CLARISSE: A most holy and mysterious event. Behold a virgin
             shall be with child and shall bring forth a son. *(sings)*
             'In my Father's house, in my Father's house.'

LENA: Clarisse, please, the ladies'!

The clock starts cuckooing.

LENA: Please, Clarisse!

RICKY enters with more glasses.

CLARISSE: Shit. Santa, where's the toilet?

RICKY slaps the clock into silence.

CLARISSE: Wait a sec here, you. Answer me. That couch ain't waterproof by the looks of it.

RICKY: Ho ho ho, let Santa go.

LENA: Clarisse!

RICKY: Hands off, hey, hands off Santa's beard!

CLARISSE: You answer me, you little— What the hell are you doing here?

RICKY: Let go! It's Christmas Eve and I'm Santa Claus.

CLARISSE: Sure, and I'm the Virgin Mary.

LENA: Clarisse, Clarisse, I feel weird again.

CLARISSE: What are you doing here? Answer.

RICKY: You're breaking my arm.

CLARISSE: Not yet, I'm not.

RICKY: You don't act like no Christian. Shit, you don't act like
                no lady!

The sound off of a car arriving.

LENA: Please, Clarisse.

CLARISSE: I'm here, Princess.

RICKY: Fuck, that hurts. Give me my face. *(grabs the beard
                and heads for the door)*

CLARISSE: Come back here, you little—

LENA: Clarisse, it hurts!

Another light on the tree burns out.

CLARISSE: I'm here, Princess, I'm here. Sit back down for a sec.

*RICKY opens the door, looks out, spins around, closes the door and runs
upstairs.*

LENA: It hurts, Clarisse. I want up.

CLARISSE: No, sweetie, no.

LENA: I want up. Please, I want up.

CLARISSE: You can't do it here. We got to get you to the hospital.

LENA: Clarisse, it hurts so bad.

All the lights on the tree goes out.

CLARISSE: Shit, Lord, this ain't no way to treat Your servant.

The clock starts cuckooing. BOO, BARBARA and JACK enter onto the porch.

LENA: Clarisse! Clarisse!

CLARISSE: I'm here, Princess.

BOO: The lights are all on.

JACK: For Christ sake, Babsy, didn't you lock the door?

BARBARA: Don't talk to me, Jack.

LENA: It hurts! Shit, it hurts!

BOO: Maybe Ma's up.

CLARISSE: Hold on, Princess. Hold on tight!

LENA screams.

BOO: *(opening the door)* That doesn't sound like Ma.

BOO, JACK and BARBARA step inside.

BARBARA: Oh my God!

CLARISSE: Shit, God. Holy shit! *(screams with LENA)*

The lights step down to black, the cuckoo stops, the sound of the toilet flushing.

END OF ACT ONE

ACT TWO

The sound of the toilet flushing and the clock cuckooing. Lights up. The scream ends and the action continues.

JACK: What is this shit?

LENA: Oh God, I hate him, Clarisse, I hate him!

JACK slaps the clock silent.

CLARISSE: Take it easy, sweetie.

BOO: Uncle Jack, it's Lena.

JACK: Hold on.

BOO: Look, it's Lena!

BARBARA: Oh my God, she's pregnant.

BOO: Lena! Lena, it's me.

JACK: Hold it, Boo.

LENA: Boo!

JACK: What the hell's going on here?

CLARISSE: Behold the Handmaid of the Lord!

LENA: Oh Boo, where've you been?

BARBARA: We went out to dinner.

JACK: Babsy, wait a minute.

BARBARA: But they gave our reservations away.

BOO: Gosh, your head's hot.

CLARISSE: Happens all the time, lady.

LENA: We been waiting so long, little sister.

BOO: Look, Auntie, it's Lena.

JACK: But who the fuck is that?

BARBARA: How are you feeling, dear?

BOO: We're here now, Lena.

LENA: I'm all right, Auntie.

CLARISSE: It'll all be okay, Princess.

JACK: Babsy, who is this person?

BARBARA: Don't talk to me, Jack.

LENA: What's the matter, Auntie?

BARBARA: Nothing.

BOO: Uncle kind of ripped Auntie's dress helping her out of
               the car.

JACK: Lucky we came back early, Babsy.

CLARISSE: Oh lady, lady, the pains are getting closer together.

BOO: Ma's not going to like this very much, Lena.

JACK: I asked if you know this woman?

BARBARA: She was the one on the porch.

LENA: I know, Boo. I'm sorry.

CLARISSE: We bring you tidings of great big joy for all mankind.

BOO: It's okay, sis.

LENA: He lied to us.

JACK: This doesn't look like good news to me, lady.

CLARISSE: But it is, it is!

BOO: What are you talking about?

LENA: We should never have fought over him.

CLARISSE: Behold a virgin shall be with child and they shall call
              him Emmanuel—

JACK: This kid's no virgin.

CLARISSE: —which being interpreted is 'God is with us.'

RICKY enters downstairs sneaking toward the door.

CLARISSE: Glory, glory, glory to God in the highest!

JACK: Can you hold that down?

BARBARA: We have noise bylaws.

JACK: We got to get her out of here. Where are the keys?

BARBARA: *(seeing RICKY)* Oh my God, Jack, look. That's our Santa suit!

LENA: Boo, don't leave.

JACK: Hold it right there, shitface.

RICKY: Ho ho ho, Santa Claus has got to go! *(runs out the open door and off)*

BOO: Wait, Uncle Jack!

JACK: Who knows what the hell else he's taken?

BOO: Forget about him.

CLARISSE: The miracle's going to happen here. Blessed be this house. *(while she sings, the action continues)*
        Jesus will be here,
        In my Father's house,
        Jesus will be here,
        In my Father's house,
        Jesus will be here,
        In my Father's house,
        And there'll be joy, joy, joy,
        Sweet joy.

JACK: I told you to can that crap.

LENA: Boo, please!

BOO: We got to get going, Uncle.

BARBARA: Oh Jack, what if she's right?

JACK: Oh fuck, he's getting into the car.

The sound of the car starting.

BOO: Uncle Jack, I forgot the keys.

JACK: College kids. *(grabs the Santa belt from the floor and exits out the front door at a run)*

BARBARA: Oh my God, Jack, be careful.

LENA: Boo, I want to talk to you.

BOO: Okay, sis, okay.

The sound of tires squealing.

BARBARA: Oh my God, Boo.

BOO: What is it, Auntie?

BARBARA: Jack's chasing after the car. It's backing up down the street. Oh God, it's swerving all over the place.

The sound of a crash.

CLARISSE: *(ends her song)* What the hell was that?

BARBARA: The big tree at the corner.

BOO: Shit. I like that tree.

BARBARA: Oh good, Jack's got him. *(she exits out front, closing the door)*

CLARISSE: How we getting to the hospital now?

BOO: Stay where you are, sis.

LENA: Forgive me, Boo? Boo?

BOO: Sure, Lena, sure.

CLARISSE: I'll phone the hospital, okay?

LENA: He lied to us, Boo. He lied. And then he left me like this.

BOO: Who left you like this, Lena?

LENA: Johnny did.

BOO: Oh shit, Lena.

CLARISSE: Excuse me. Excuse me, kid.

LENA: I hate him, Boo.

BOO: Lena, the guy was dead long ago. You hear me, Lena? He's dead.

CLARISSE: Where is it?

LENA: Really? Good.

CLARISSE: Hey! Where's your telephone?

BOO: What? It's probably in the crisper.

LENA: I hate him. I hate him so much.

BOO: Here. Hold her. I'll go check. *(she exits to the kitchen)*

CLARISSE: Hold still, Lena. Hold still. *(sings)* 'Jesus will be here.'

The clock starts cuckooing. BOO enters and slaps it silent.

BOO: It's not there. It wasn't in the dishwasher either.

CLARISSE: What is it with that crummy clock?

BOO: Uncle Buck's hunting trophy. From the first house he ever flipped.

LENA: Boo, wait. I got to talk to you.

BOO: Sis, I'll be right back. I got to ask Ma where the phone is.

LENA: Is Momma here, Boo?

BOO: I'd better warn her about your condition.

LENA: Don't tell her, Boo, please.

BOO: She'll see it right off, sis.

LENA: Does she hate me, Boo?

BOO: She's your mother.

LENA: I don't want her to see me like this.

BOO: She wants to see you, Lena. You're all she talks about.

LENA: It'll kill her, Boo.

BOO: It's not that easy, sis.

LENA: Make her forgive me, Boo.

BOO: Look, I'll be right back.

CLARISSE: Okay by me. We ain't moving nowhere.

BOO exits upstairs.

CLARISSE: She's coming right back, Princess. Hold still.

LENA: Momma said Johnny would hurt me.

CLARISSE: A wise woman, your mother.

LENA: She told me so. She's not like you.

CLARISSE: No, she ain't like me at all, Princess.

LENA: You're good to me. You forgive me.

CLARISSE: Honey, I got to admit it, I'm the best. Here, sip on this.

LENA: Make her forgive me, Clarisse.

BARBARA, JACK and RICKY, tied awkwardly with the belt, enter the front door.

RICKY: Let go, you old bugger. You can't fucking treat Father
            Christmas this way.

JACK: Shut the fuck up!

BARBARA: I don't like him talking that way, Jack.

RICKY: You're really pissing me off, dad. No presents for you
            two.

JACK: Go call the cops, Babsy.

BARBARA: This is so embarrassing. I'm sure I saw Missus Jones
            peeking out her drapes.

JACK: Come on, Babsy, move it.

BARBARA: I hope nobody else saw us, Jack. They won't credit
            what she says.

JACK: Snap out of it, Babsy

BARBARA *gets the telephone out of the closet.*

RICKY: You're hurting me, Dad. Why the fuck are you people
            so rough? I don't like it.

JACK: You shut your trap or I'll really take care of you.

RICKY: Are we talking naughty and nice?

JACK: You little pervert.

RICKY: Ah, come on, guy, you're the one with the leather belt.
            Ow! Goodwill towards men already.

JACK: Out of the way, Babsy. *(throws RICKY into the closet and closes the door)* I need to wash my hands.

BARBARA: Jack, I left some presents in there.

JACK: Plug the thing in and phone the cops, Babsy.

BARBARA: But the presents, Jack, the presents are in there.

JACK: Oh all right. *(opens the closet door)* Stay where you are.

RICKY: Hey, Dad, let's be buddies.

LENA: Clarisse, Clarisse, it's hurting again.

RICKY: Let me go, Dad. I'll be good. I promise.

CLARISSE: You're going to be okay, Princess.

RICKY: Here, Daddy. *(starts to hand out the packages)*

JACK: Stop calling me that, you little shit. No way are we related.

CLARISSE: It's supposed to happen this way. *(sings quietly)*
'There'll be joy, joy, joy,
Sweet joy—'

BARBARA: I asked you not to sing that.

RICKY: Come on, old man. Peace. I'll make it up to you. Hey, I can be a real good boy. *(holds out the jewellery box)*

JACK: Shut up. Here, Babsy. Look after it this time.

BARBARA: How did that get in there?

RICKY: Come on, guy, Santa's got goodies to deliver.

JACK: Shut your filthy trap. Christ almighty, is that all?

BARBARA: I think so.

RICKY: Oh Daddy, I got one more for you. (*kisses JACK on the mouth*)

JACK: Get off of me, you little shithead!

BARBARA: Jack!

JACK slams the closet door closed and leans against it. The toilet flushes.

JACK: I need to disinfect my lips.

BARBARA: Did he bite you, Jack?

JACK: Shit, call the cops, Babsy.

BOO: (*enters downstairs*) Auntie, Auntie!

LENA: Clarisse?

BARBARA: What is it, Boo?

CLARISSE: Hold still, sweetie.

LENA: Let me up, Clarisse.

BOO: Ma won't tell me where the phone is.

LENA: I want to sit up.

JACK: Fuck, I'll call them myself.

LENA screams.

CLARISSE: Hey, folks! Excuse me, folks!

BOO: I got to call an ambulance, Uncle Jack.

CLARISSE: Hey, excuse me but I think it's too late!

BARBARA: What? Oh not on my rug!

JACK: Oh God. Come on. Get her out of here.

BOO: Uncle, she can't travel now. Not like this. You want to
                kill her?

JACK: Well, then take her upstairs. Come on. Help her. Up
                up. You. Move it.

CLARISSE: Okay, okay.

JACK: Move it, Boo.

BOO: Come on, Lena, walk with us.

LENA: I got to go, Boo. I got to go.

BARBARA: How are you feeling, dear?

LENA screams.

CLARISSE: Come on, Princess, everything's going to be cool.

BARBARA: Oh God, Jack.

BOO: Auntie, come help.

BARBARA: I don't know about babies, Boo.

BOO: But you got to get Ma out of the bathroom, Auntie.

LENA: I got to go now.

BOO: We'll need the sink, the hot water, Auntie. Isn't that right?

CLARISSE: How the hell should I know? I take precautions.

BARBARA: Someone should call the hospital.

JACK: What a sorry bunch of women.

LENA: Clarisse, please. Please.

CLARISSE: Come on, let's move it.

BOO: Auntie?

BARBARA: Let me call the hospital first, Boo. Then I'll come talk to her.

CLARISSE: Time is of the essence, lady.

BOO and CLARISSE exit with LENA upstairs.

BARBARA: I know what time it is. Jack, I'm calling the hospital.

RICKY: Dial nine one one. Nine one one.

JACK: After I call the cops.

BARBARA: Jack, wait. Wait a minute.

JACK: Time is of the essence, Babsy.

BARBARA: Do we have to call the police, Jack?

JACK: What are you on about?

BARBARA: You know how they look at us.

JACK: We got a problem in this cupboard.

BARBARA: The neighbours. If they see a police car parked in front of our house—

JACK: Babsy, our car back-ended the oldest tree on the block.

BARBARA: I'm sure they'll understand if we just explain it to them.

RICKY: Ya, be reasonable, guy.

JACK: How you going to explain this? You see their eyes glaze over every day.

RICKY: What about the hospital?

BARBARA: Jack, I just want to make friends. They like the house now.

JACK: Babsy, we shouldn't care about those buggers.

BARBARA: Couldn't we just take him to the station ourselves?

JACK: Our car ain't going no place, babe. It's a write-off.

BARBARA: A taxi. We could call a taxi.

RICKY: I get to go for a taxi ride!

JACK: (*pounds the closet door for silence and gets it*) Babsy, this little creep broke into our house.

BARBARA: I know, Jack, but they'll say it's our own fault.

JACK: He had your necklace.

RICKY: I gave it back, man.

BARBARA: He gave it back, Jack. And what about Lena? What if the police take Lena away too?

JACK: Now why would they do that?

BARBARA: We don't know what kind of trouble she's in.

JACK: It seems pretty obvious.

BARBARA: Jack, poor Martha's seeing her daughter for the first time in months. It might kill her if the police took Lena away.

JACK: No such luck, Babsy.

The sound of the toilet flushing making an ugly noise in the pipes down into the basement.

BARBARA: We have to wait. Promise me we'll wait.

JACK: What the fuck is with them pipes? Shit. This is crazy.

BARBARA: Jack, Jack, you're the one who's always talking about property values.

JACK: All right, we'll wait. So where the hell's the key to this door?

BARBARA: It's on the hook in the kitchen. *(exits to kitchen)*

RICKY: You can't keep me in here, Dad. It ain't legal.

JACK: Just watch me.

RICKY: Sure, you caught me fair and square, but you got to turn me over to the cops.

JACK: Just watch me.

RICKY: You'll be sorry, Dad. I'm the ghost of Christmas. I can pass through walls.

BARBARA: *(enters)* Here's the key, Jack.

JACK: I think you're Ricky Raccoon and you're going to cut the crap. *(locks the closet door)*

RICKY: Come on, Dad. Don't do that. Let me go.

BARBARA: *(takes the key)* Jack, do you smell something funny?

BOO: *(enters downstairs)* Auntie. Auntie!

BARBARA: I'm coming, Boo. I was just wondering. What about the presents?

RICKY: That's my job! Ho ho ho—

JACK *pounds a silence.*

BOO: What are you talking about?

BARBARA: There's nothing for Lena.

BOO: Is the ambulance coming?

JACK: We haven't got through yet.

BOO: Try again, Uncle, please. Auntie, Ma's got her blankets with her in the bathtub.

BARBARA: She can't stay in there like that.

BOO: She won't believe Lena's here.

JACK: So get Lena to talk to her.

BOO: Lena's kind of occupied, Uncle.

BARBARA: Jack, what should I do?

BOO: Auntie, you're her sister. She'll listen.

BARBARA: Didn't you hear what she said to me before, Boo? She thinks I'm full of it.

BOO: She just said that because she was pissed off.

JACK: Ya, babe, we all know better. She's the one who's full of shit.

BARBARA: Jack, please.

JACK: Take pity on her, Babsy. Her and her rotten life.

BARBARA: I just wanted her to realize the kind of woman Lena is now.

JACK: Say you're sorry, Babsy. Even old cold Fish should see it's kind of beside the point right now.

BOO: She's real upset. I could hear her start to cry soon as she heard the preacher lady going 'Glory glory glory!'

BARBARA: Preacher lady? What's she doing? What's that woman doing up there?

JACK: She's all by herself, Babsy. Did you leave your turquoise shit unlocked?

BARBARA: Oh my God, Jack.

JACK: Go on. I'll do the hospital.

BARBARA exits upstairs.

JACK: Hold it, Booster. You better call the hospital. They might want to know her condition. I mean if she's so far gone.

RICKY: Help! I'm real far gone too.

BOO: What's going on?

177

JACK: I've got that fairy Santa Claus in the closet.

BOO: That's not funny. Let him out.

JACK: That little housebreaker? He's your little boy friend, isn't he? The one you're so hot and chocolatey with?

RICKY: There's a really funny smell in here, guys.

BOO: So what if he is?

JACK: That's a faggot in there, little girl.

RICKY: It really is hard to breathe.

JACK: He's not exactly the marrying kind, kiddo.

BOO: Uncle, I got to call Saint Joseph's. Where's the phone book?

RICKY: It's in here! It's in here!

JACK: Come on, Boo, you can do better than that even from the bush Indians.

BOO: Uncle Jack, the hospital?

JACK: You turn your back and he's casing the joint. He had your Aunt's present all wrapped up.

BOO: The hospital, Uncle.

RICKY: Boo, nine one one! Nine one one!

JACK: *(pounds a silence)* This piece of shit. What do you
             think he was doing here?

BOO: Lena. He brought her back. Like he said.

RICKY: Ya, Dad, I brought her back.

JACK: Wake up, little girl. He's a thief. Is that what you want
             out of life?

BOO: Uncle, let me by. I want the phone.

JACK: He's not getting out, Boo.

BOO: Let me by, please.

JACK: You're not very bright for a college girl.

BOO: Let go of me. Let go.

JACK: But I guess brains aren't everything, are they, Booster?

BOO: Get your hands off me, Uncle Buck! Off!

The clock cuckoos once.

JACK: I'm sorry. I just don't want you to get hurt.

BOO: You got a shitty way of showing it.

JACK: I'm sorry, Boo.

RICKY makes a raspberry.

BOO: So where's the stupid key?

JACK: Your aunt has it. I'm sorry, Boo.

RICKY: Hey, Booboo, nine one one. Nine one one!

JACK: Will you shut the fuck up? *(pounds the door)* Christ
               alive, where's my bottle. *(exits to kitchen)*

BOO: *(dials the emergency number)* Hello? I need Saint
               Joseph's quick. I got a woman in labour here. I don't
               know how long. It's my sister. Thanks but hurry.
               Hurry.

CLARISSE: *(enters downstairs)* Hey! Hey, Boo! The Princess wants
               you.

BOO: I'm on the phone here.

CLARISSE: Time is of the essence, kiddo.

BOO: Here. Come on, you take over.

JACK enters, now with beer.

BOO: Tell the operator where we are. *(exits upstairs)*

CLARISSE: So where are we? I gave the cabby my note with the
               address.

JACK: Give it here.

RICKY: Help! Help me, Church Lady!

CLARISSE: What's that racket?

JACK: Santa got stuck in the chimney.

RICKY: He's got me locked in the vacuum cleaner room.

JACK: You know him?

CLARISSE: Santa Claus?

JACK: Don't be smart. *(hangs up phone)*

CLARISSE: Mister, the hospital. You hung up.

JACK: I asked you a question.

CLARISSE: I seen him around.

JACK: Did he bring you here tonight? I didn't think so. You just tumbled on the address?

CLARISSE: Her Momma left the address at the Mission.

JACK: That was months ago. You knew we were looking for her.

CLARISSE: Arise and take the young child and His mother for Herod will seek to destroy Him.

JACK: Just a goddamn minute here.

CLARISSE: Hey, mister, there's a miracle going on up there!

JACK: You came here for money but you're getting shit.

CLARISSE: Mister, you're her folks.

The telephone starts ringing.

JACK: Us Bucks can't be taken.

CLARISSE: Answer the thing, why don't you?

JACK: You talk pretty funny for a tired-out streetwalker.

CLARISSE: Have some respect.

JACK: I know about you.

CLARISSE: You don't know my life.

JACK: You pimped that poor kid to your johns.

CLARISSE: You don't know shit. The Lord offered me this glori-
               ous, glorious street to walk.

RICKY: Pray for me! Pray for me, Church Lady!

CLARISSE: Oh ye of little faith. Already was she with child when
               I met her. No living man had touched her. He died
               and rose again from the dead and—

JACK: Don't give me that holy ghost bullshit.

CLARISSE: I see it coming now. I see it now! The spirit of the
               Lord is upon her. Glory, glory—

JACK: She's a little slut.

CLARISSE: Like a beast of the field you witness the coming of the
               child back into this world of flesh and yet you don't
               know shit.

RICKY: No shit!

The toilet flushes and another more horrible noise travels the pipes to the basement.

JACK: What the fuck is going on?

CLARISSE: You going to answer that thing?

JACK turns and picks up the phone.

CLARISSE: I got to go serve the child and his mother.

JACK: Wait a minute. You're not going near my niece again.

CLARISSE: Let me go. Let go.

JACK: Come on, out with you.

In their struggle the telephone is ripped from its line.

CLARISSE: I'm sorry, I didn't mean—

JACK: Oh Jesus, shit! Well, I don't mean this either.

CLARISSE: No. I can't go. No! Please.

RICKY: What's going on out there? Hello?

JACK: Come on. That's not going to do you any good now. Let go.

CLARISSE: You got to let me stay. Let me go! Please. This is what I was born to do. She's my friend. I got to help her bring this life into the world.

BARBARA enters downstairs.

JACK: You can't help anybody.

BARBARA: What's going on?

JACK: I'm showing the lady out.

BARBARA: Are you crazy, Clarisse? You can't go now. Please, Lena's
                 asking for you.

JACK: The lady has urgent business elsewhere.

BARBARA: No, you have to come upstairs. Jack, make her stay.

JACK: Babsy, do you know what you're saying?

BARBARA: Jack, Lena will not lie still.

CLARISSE: I'm coming.

BARBARA: I'm afraid she'll hurt herself.

BARBARA and CLARISSE exit upstairs.

RICKY: How do? Anybody there?

JACK: Shut up, shitface.

RICKY: I haven't had a drink all night!

JACK pounds the door.

RICKY: Hey, Dad, unlax. I give up.

JACK: You disgust me, you silly little—

RICKY: I said 'Uncle,' Uncle. Honest Injun.

JACK: Do you want to die? *(throws the phone against the wall, smashing it)*

RICKY: You mean like your wife's hair?

JACK tries to open the door.

RICKY: Hey, I think somebody locked the door, man.

The sound of the toilet flushing and the pipes protesting all the way to the basement. JACK goes to the foot of the stairs.

RICKY: Hey, man, what's the racket? Are you there, Dad?

BOO: *(enters downstairs)* Uncle, Uncle, what about the ambulance?

JACK: Tonto would like to get out. I need your aunt's keys.

BOO: But what about the ambulance, Uncle?

The sound of the toilet again flushing upstairs and again the pipes protest.

JACK: Will you tell her to quit flushing that thing! Them pipes are old.

BOO: She likes the sound of running water, Uncle. It sounds like the river at home.

JACK: I want them keys.

BOO: Don't come up. I'll get them. What about the ambulance?

RICKY: It's not coming, it's not coming.

BOO: What's he on about?

JACK: They said to use a cab. It's bad out there tonight.
             Trouble all over the place.

BOO: So you got a cab coming or not?

JACK: They're really busy.

BOO: Uncle, Lena's in trouble up there. Do you hear me?
             She's in trouble.

JACK: That woman. She fucked the phone line.

RICKY: Liar, liar, pants on fire!

JACK: You shut up, you little closet case!

BOO: Can you fix it? Uncle, get with it.

RICKY: I can, I can! I'm good with screwdrivers.

JACK pounds a silence. The flush and the pipes again.

BOO: Uncle, Ma's the only one knows about birthing
             stuff—

JACK: And she won't come out of the fucking water closet!

BOO: Auntie's trying to talk her out, but Uncle, we got to get
             help. Lena don't look good.

RICKY: I'll go, I'll go!

JACK pounds a silence.

BOO: Uncle, maybe that makes sense. Let him go for help.
                Please.

JACK: He's not going no place. I'll go down to the main drag.
                (puts on his overcoat) See what I can flag down.

BOO: It's raining out there, Uncle. It'll be icy.

JACK: I need the fucking air. *(exits out, slamming the door)*

BOO watches him go.

RICKY: Hello? Anybody there? You hoo! You who? How do?
                Ho ho ho—

*BOO gets the key out of her pocket and opens the closet door, leaving the
key in the lock.*

RICKY: Shit. What a stinking hole. I'm closet-phobic, you
                know.

BOO: Come on, Ricky, get going before he comes back.

RICKY: What? What? Oh my ears are ringing.

BOO: Go. Go. Understand. My Uncle wants to kill you.

RICKY: Why's he so uptight, babe? I was just having some
                fun.

BOO: He's a serious man, Ricky.

RICKY: Can't he see I'm too cute to die?

BOO: He probably sees you're too silly to live.

RICKY: I'm wounded.

BOO: Cut the comedy, Ricky.

RICKY: But what's life without laughs?

BOO: This house, I guess.

RICKY: Hey, this is a big place.

BOO: Come on, Ricky.

RICKY: I don't get the guided tour?

BOO: I can't help you if he comes back. My sister's having a
            baby upstairs.

RICKY: Hey, you can't blame that one on me.

BOO: Come on, you better change. You can't go out on the
            streets in that outfit.

RICKY: I like me this way. I might attract a better clientele.

BOO: What did you do with your clothes?

RICKY: These are my clothes.

BOO: Is that them over there? Under the tree.

RICKY: Christmas presents for me?

BOO: Come on, Ricky.

RICKY: Hey, these look used!

CLARISSE: *(off)* Boo! Boo!

BOO: Hurry up. Come on. *(throws his pants and shoes into the basement)*

RICKY: What are you doing?

BOO: Go on down.

RICKY: Where have I heard that one before?

BOO: Go on. Go out the back way after you change.

BARBARA: *(off)* Boo, please come up here! Boo!

RICKY: Hey, Boo!

BOO: What is it?

RICKY: Are we still on for boxing? Boxing Day at the Donut Queen?

BOO: I don't know. I got to get them back to the bush now.

RICKY: The bush? Oh I like the sound of that. Can I come too?

BOO: I don't think Ma would go for your company.

RICKY: Oh, she could be my momma, too. I'm easy to love.

BOO: We're going to have enough trouble with one baby needing looking after.

RICKY: I'm no trouble. Believe it or not, I'm good in the bushes.

BOO: Oh brother!

RICKY: Oh sis!

BARBARA: *(on the stairs)* Boo? Boo, where are you?

BOO: Hurry up.

RICKY: There's a bad smell down there, Boo.

BOO: Go on.

RICKY: Hey, Boo, I'm not kidding. This hole smells like a sewer. Oh, Santa Claus is so sad, Boo, he's committing sewer-cide.

BOO: I'm sorry, Ricky. Thanks for bringing her back. *(exits upstairs)* Here I am, Auntie.

RICKY: *(picks up his jacket and hat)* Ah poop! Women! *(exits into the basement)*

BARBARA: *(enters downstairs, hearing the basement door close)* Jack? Jack, is that you?

The clock cuckoos. BARBARA slaps it silent. She checks the basement door.

BARBARA: Jack?

The tree sputters to light again, drawing BARBARA to kneel down beside it. She adjusts the manger and finds the Christmas star inside. The sound off of a car arriving. She picks the star up and cradles it. JACK returns, entering from the street.

JACK: I finally got a taxi here.

BARBARA: Wait a minute, Jack. Don't go up yet.

JACK: I'm not sure he'll wait.

BARBARA: She's having it. She's having the baby.

JACK: Maybe we can stop it.

BARBARA: Jack, listen to me. Wait. Listen. It's so amazing.

JACK: Are you okay? You're shaking.

BARBARA: I'm fine, Jack. I'm fine. You should see the way she
             has to push. She has to push so hard. She's shiny with
             sweat, Jack.

JACK: I'll take your word for it, Babsy.

BARBARA: I could never do that, Jack.

JACK: What is it? What is it, Babsy?

BARBARA: I want it, Jack. I want that baby.

JACK: Get a hold of it, Babsy.

BARBARA: I want that baby. You saw what she is. She can't take
             care of it.

JACK: It's not even born yet.

BARBARA: We can take care of it. We can give it a home.
             Everything we never had.

JACK: You're not going to give up on this.

BARBARA: Isn't that what we're here for, Jack? Our son will grow
               up as good as anybody. Our baby, Jack. We'll show the
               whole neighbourhood we can raise a family too.

JACK: Oh Babsy, I don't know.

BARBARA: Jack, God is giving us this chance.

JACK: God's got nothing to do with this, Babsy.

BARBARA: Please, Jack, get me that baby.

JACK: Shit, Babsy.

BARBARA: Oh Jack. *(kisses him)*

JACK: Will it make you happy?

BARBARA: Jack, it will make me happy. I'll be smiling dollars.

JACK: But what if she won't give it up.

BARBARA: But we're her family, Jack. It's not like it's giving it up.

JACK: What about Martha?

BARBARA: Fuck Martha. I'm the one whose house this is. I make
               the decisions here.

JACK: Oh Babsy, baby. I guess it would be better for the kid.

BARBARA: To have stuff. Not to go without. To be really loved.

JACK: To be somebody. To be able to have what you want.

BARBARA: When you want it. I want this baby, Jack. It'll make
               me happy. It'll be ours. Our baby, Jack. I promise you.
               Our baby will make us both happy.

JACK: I don't know, Babsy.

BARBARA: Remember how happy we used to be. Big Buck
               remembers, doesn't he?

They kiss. CLARISSE enters slowly downstairs.

JACK: We can give Lena money. She can go to school. She
               could still maybe make something out of herself. She
               could bounce back.

BARBARA: Imagine how friendly everyone will be?

CLARISSE: I'm sorry.

BARBARA: We were just talking.

CLARISSE: Excuse me.

BARBARA: What's wrong?

JACK: Come on, what's the scoop?

CLARISSE: It's a girl.

JACK: Ha. I'll tell that fucking taxi to wait! *(exits out the front
               door)*

BARBARA: A girl?

CLARISSE: A girl.

BARBARA: What's the matter?

CLARISSE: It's supposed to be a boy.

BARBARA: Is she all right? Is she all right?

CLARISSE: Lady, it's supposed to be a boy.

BARBARA: Tell me if she's all right.

The sound off of the cab departing.

CLARISSE: How should I know? She's bleeding a whole lot.

BARBARA: Bleeding? How could the baby be bleeding?

CLARISSE: The baby's okay. I guess. Crying a lot. The old lady's got her. What a mess. But Lena's bleeding. The Princess is bleeding. The kid's trying to bandage her up sort of.

BARBARA: *(calling out the front door)* Jack! Jack!

CLARISSE: She looks awful pale.

BARBARA: There's a taxi out there somewhere. *(exits upstairs)*

CLARISSE: *(by the tree)* For unto you is born this day in the city a child. *(sings)* 'In my Father's house. In my Father's house.' Our Father, who art in heaven. Fuck, Lena, what is this? This shithouse. It's not supposed to go this way. Oh God, why's it going this way? She's highly favoured, blessed among women. She is. Shit, she is.

BOO: (*enters downstairs*) Uncle Jack! Uncle! Where's my Uncle Buck?

CLARISSE: What's going on?

BOO: We got to get her to the hospital quick.

CLARISSE: Your aunt said there's a taxi. How is she?

The sound of the taxi returning.

BOO: Can't see nothing.

CLARISSE: How's the Princess?

BOO: Wait a minute.

CLARISSE exits upstairs.

BOO: Here comes one now. Uncle! Uncle Jack! So where the hell have you been?

JACK: (*enters the front door*) We turned the cab around. The road's slippery as shit.

BOO: We got to hurry. Lena's real bad.

·JACK: Ya, well, how's the baby?

BOO: The baby's good, I guess. Ma's holding her.

JACK: Your Ma's awake?

BOO: Soon as she heard the cry, she was off the pot and on the job.

JACK: No shit?

CLARISSE: *(calls downstairs)* Hurry up! Come on, you guys, Lena's passed out.

JACK and BOO exit upstairs. RICKY enters, still in the Santa suit, screwdriver in hand, from the basement. The sound of the taxi leaving.

JACK: *(off)* Out of the way.

CLARISSE: *(off)* Here's a blanket.

JACK: *(off)* What about the shoes?

RICKY watches from the living room as CLARISSE, JACK carrying LENA, and BOO enter down into the hall.

BOO: Careful, Uncle.

JACK: I am being careful. Open that door.

CLARISSE: I'm way ahead of you. Oh shit, the bugger's gone.

JACK: I told him we'd be right out.

CLARISSE: Hey, look, those his tail lights? *(exits out front)*

JACK: Ah shit.

RICKY slips into the closet as JACK comes and sits LENA on the couch.

JACK: Look out. Out of my way. Move it. *(exits out front)*

LENA: Boo?

BOO: Right here, sis. Don't try to talk.

LENA: I'm cold, Boo.

BOO: It's the middle of winter, sis.

LENA: You're funny.

BOO: Glad you think so.

LENA: You're like Johnny. All that history stuff in your head.

BOO: Don't talk about him, Lena.

LENA: Don't let it make you lonely, Boo.

BOO: Come on, Lena, keep still.

LENA: It's just a bad story.

BOO: I know, sis.

LENA: It made him too lonely to stay. Do you believe in it, Boo? Johnny didn't believe in Indians.

BOO: It's kind of hard not to, sis.

LENA: I forgive him now. They treat you like a ghost.

BOO: What are you on about, Lena?

LENA: I saw it, Boo. All the white faces and nobody believes in ghosts.

The toilet flushes and the pipes scream.

LENA: But you, you have to. Take care of her. Take care of my baby.

BOO: You lazy? You take care of her yourself.

LENA: Please, Boo. Tell her the story.

BOO: I don't know babies, Lena.

LENA: You know about this baby, Boo. Like Clarisse says. This baby is a gift.

BOO: It ain't exactly what I wanted for Christmas, sis.

LENA: A new story, Boo. Name her Barbara. A little Boo.

JACK enters the front door.

BOO: Oh shit, sis.

JACK: Okay, your friend's holding the taxi. Come on. Upsy-daisy.

LENA: I'm not going to be here.

JACK: Can't you girls can it till you get in the cab?

LENA: I got to go. He's waiting for me. Now.

JACK: You bet he is.

BOO: No, Lena, you got something better to think about now.

LENA: We're going to be happy now.

BOO: Shit, Lena, you can't do this.

JACK: Bring the baby. (*exits out front, carrying LENA*)

BOO exits up the stairs. RICKY comes out of the closet and peers out the front window, then hides behind the tree as JACK comes back in.

JACK: Babsy! Babsy, where are you?

BARBARA: (*off*) I'm up here, Jack.

JACK: Come on, Babsy, where's the kid?

BARBARA: (*enters downstairs*) I'm sorry, Jack.

JACK: What is it?

BARBARA: Martha won't let me have her.

JACK: You're kidding.

BARBARA: She wouldn't even let me touch her.

JACK: Well, let's just take it from her.

BARBARA: Jack, I think she knows. She called me a paleface. She said I wasn't going to steal any babies.

JACK: The woman's off her stool, Babsy.

BARBARA: She took the baby and locked themselves in the john again. Boo's trying to talk to her through the keyhole.

JACK: I got to get rid of that lock. Wait here, Babsy.

JACK *exits upstairs. The sound of the taxi's horn.* BARBARA *goes to look out the door. The horn again.*

BARBARA: Jack! Jack!

The sound of the taxi departing.

BARBARA: Oh no. Jack!

RICKY *sneaks closer to the door.*

BARBARA: (*at the foot of the stairs*) Jack, the cab's gone. It's gone!

JACK: (*off*) Hold onto it, Babsy!

BARBARA: The cab's gone, Jack.

JACK: (*enters downstairs*) Fuck. I almost busted my shoulder.

BARBARA: What happened, Jack?

JACK: That fucking Boo's in there with them now too and she wouldn't let me in!

BARBARA: Jack, maybe we better forget it.

JACK: What?

BARBARA: If she knows about the baby—

JACK: Fuck, Babsy, we're in luck. Lena's dying. We'll have to take care of the kid.

BARBARA: Jack, that's not true.

JACK: I'm sorry, Babsy. Get a hold on it. The Boo's talking to Martha now, trying to get through that shitty skull of hers. It'll work out. You better go talk to her too.

BARBARA: She won't listen to me. Not now.

JACK: Babsy, there's no way she could know. Listen to me. No way. Now go on. You're her sister. Or did you forget?

BARBARA: You know I tried to, Jack. You know how I tried.

JACK: Like your family was dead. Shit, Babsy, we got to play the rules. We want that kid with its mother, I better get another fucking cab. (*exits out front*)

The clock starts cuckooing. BARBARA turns toward it but stops when she sees RICKY.

RICKY: Ho ho ho, little girl. (*slaps the clock silent*) Father Christmas at your service.

BARBARA: How did you get out?

RICKY: Is that what you really want for Christmas?

BARBARA: Please. I told him to let you go.

RICKY: You must be a really good girl, Babsy.

BARBARA: Why don't you just go?

RICKY: So Santa will really fix your cuckoo clock for you. (*takes the clock down from the wall*)

201

BARBARA: Don't touch that. That's Jack's.

RICKY: See how good Santa Claus is with screwdrivers? Here
               you go. Merry Christmas.

BARBARA: Please. Just go.

RICKY: This is really what you're getting for Christmas. Take
               it. Take it, little Princess.

BARBARA: Stop it. Just leave me alone. I'll call the police.

RICKY: This is what you get for being such a good little
               Indian.

BARBARA: No. No, I wanted the baby.

RICKY: You're cuckoo, lady. You can't own babies.

BARBARA: You just stay where you are—

She turns to run but RICKY throws the clock and spooks her.

BARBARA: Get away from me. Go on. Let me go. Let go.

*The clock cuckoos into silence as RICKY grabs and wrestles BARBARA
into the closet.*

BARBARA: Help! Help! You can't do this to me! Help!

*The toilet flushes and the pipes scream. RICKY locks the closet door,
takes the key and the clock, and exits upstairs.*

BARBARA: Let me out! Let me out! Let me out out out!

JACK enters the front door.

JACK: I had to pay the bugger to wait. Babsy! Babsy, where are you? You up there, Babsy?

BARBARA: Jack? Jack, wait! I'm here! I'm here!

JACK: Babsy? Where the fuck are you?

BARBARA: Come on, Jack, get me out.

RICKY enters downstairs, carrying the bundled baby, and exits out front.

BARBARA: Get me out of here!

JACK: What's going on?

BARBARA: That boy. That kid in the Santa suit.

JACK: Fuck. I forgot about him. What happened?

BARBARA: He locked me in here, you jerk.

JACK: How'd he get loose?

BARBARA: I don't care, I don't care, get me out of here!

The sound of the taxi departing.

JACK: Babsy, haven't you got the key?

BARBARA: Get me out of here, Jack.

JACK: But Babsy, the key's not here. Who's got the key?

BARBARA: Hurry up! Hurry up! Hurry up! Hurry up!

JACK: Shit, that kid could be cleaning us out.

BARBARA: Get me out of here, Jack.

JACK: Hold your horses, Babsy.

BOO: *(enters downstairs)* I finally got them out of the john. What a relief! Uncle, I wish I had your bladder.

BARBARA: Hurry up! Hurry up!

JACK: Your little fag friend locked your aunt in the closet.

BOO: You're kidding. How do you like it, Auntie?

BARBARA: It's not funny, Boo.

BOO: But I sent him packing long ago.

BARBARA: Get me out of here! *(pounds so hard the door, most of its screws already removed by RICKY, pops open and hangs on its hinges)*

JACK: Babsy, are you okay?

BARBARA: Leave me alone. Leave me alone. I want to see the baby.

BOO: Auntie, wait, slow down. She's snoozing. Don't wake her up.

BARBARA: I want to see the baby. *(exits upstairs)*

BOO: But I finally got them quieted down.

JACK: I got a cab waiting for the hospital.

BOO: But she seems okay.

JACK: She should be with her mother.

BOO: I don't see no cab, Uncle.

JACK: Oh hell. I gave the guy fifty bucks. I told him we'd be bringing a baby.

BARBARA: (*enters downstairs*) Jack! Jack! Jack! Jack! The baby's gone. The baby's gone!

JACK: What are you talking about?

BARBARA: Someone's stolen my baby!

BOO: I just left them for a—

JACK: Shit. Babsy, get a hold on it.

BOO exits upstairs.

BARBARA: Don't touch me, Jack.

JACK: Come on, babe, it's not my fault.

BARBARA: Nothing's your fault, is it? Nothing can be blamed on you. I'm the one. I know it. It's all my fault, isn't it? I can't even keep track of a baby. I just lose track. Why do you trust me at all, Jack? Why? You shouldn't be giving me expensive gifts. Here. Take it back. *(tries to give him back the jewellery box)*

JACK: No, Babsy, get a hold on it.

BARBARA: Take it back. Take it back.

JACK: No, Babsy—

BARBARA: *(tries to give back all the Christmas gifts)* Take it all back, all of this stuff. You know how expensive it is. You know I can't keep track. You keep track. Take it back, Jack. You can keep track of everything. You're so in control, it hurts.

JACK: What the fuck's the matter with you?

BARBARA: And look at this place. What a mess. I made the whole mess myself. How can I expect company when I'm such a rotten housekeeper? How can I, Jack? I'm ashamed of me, aren't you?

BOO: *(enters downstairs)* It's true. The baby's gone.

BARBARA: I can't even keep track of a baby, Jack.

JACK: Babsy, shut up. It's not your fault.

BOO: What's the story, Uncle?

JACK: Nothing. I'm sorry, Babs. I'm sorry.

BARBARA: That kid. That kid in our Santa suit. He did it. He did it all.

BOO: Oh, come on. Why would he do this?

JACK: Then who did? Santa Claus?

BOO: Ah shit.

JACK: Wait. I'd better go with you.

BOO: I don't want you anywhere near me, Uncle Buck. You
            better get the police.

BARBARA: But Martha had the baby.

BOO: Ma's asleep. She's got that stupid cuckoo clock in her
            arms.

JACK: What?

BOO: I know where the little bugger lives. *(exits out the front
            door, leaving it open)*

BARBARA: What will I tell her, Jack?

JACK: What you talking about, Babsy?

BARBARA: What would you do if someone took your grandchild?
            I couldn't bear it, Jack. I couldn't. How does she do it,
            Jack?

JACK: Babsy, you're just upset. Let me get you a drink.

BARBARA: No, Jack, I have to think.

JACK: Come on, Babsy. Come to your Big Buck.

BARBARA: Don't, Jack. No. How am I going to clean up this
             mess? Oh God, how did this happen? I can't let any-
             one see the room like this.

JACK: Let it be for now, Babsy.

BARBARA: Martha would know what to do. She's good at clean-
             ing. She'll help if I ask. Don't you think so? If I say
             Lena's okay?

JACK: I don't know. Shouldn't you let her sleep? Babsy, wait.

BARBARA exits upstairs. The Christmas tree bursts into flames.

JACK: Oh shit. Babsy! Babsy! Oh fuck.

*JACK manages to smother the flames using the Christmas presents. There
is a lot of smoke. CLARISSE enters onto the porch.*

CLARISSE: Hello? Hey, hello! Anybody there! What's going on?

JACK: *(meets her at the door)* Well, what the fuck are you
             doing back here?

CLARISSE: Oh shit. You scared me, mister.

JACK: Well?

CLARISSE: I bring you tidings, mister, bad news. Great big bad.

JACK: So what's the scoop? Where's Lena?

CLARISSE: With her Johnny I guess.

JACK: What the hell are you talking about?

CLARISSE: Shit, I hope not. I mean, mister, she sort of died in the cab. I'm real sorry.

JACK: Sort of died.

CLARISSE: She got real cold real sudden, mister. She got that face on her. I'm real sorry.

JACK: Face? What are you talking about?

CLARISSE: I'm sorry but I just had to get out of there. That look on her face. I had to get away from it. I jumped out of the cab at a corner. I'm really sorry, mister.

JACK: Well, I guess she didn't need you any more, did she? Wait a minute. Where are you going?

CLARISSE: How should I know? I don't know how the story's supposed to go. *(exits into the night)*

JACK: Wait a minute. Shit shit shit shit.

BARBARA enters downstairs.

BARBARA: Jack? Jack, what's going on?

JACK: Shit, Babs, the tree caught fire. It's okay. I put it out. Those lights were old.

BARBARA: This is awful, Jack.

JACK: Never mind. I'll clean it up. What a mess. The phone's fucked too.

BARBARA: How did this happen, Jack?

JACK: Short circuit, I guess. I don't know.

BARBARA: What did we do wrong? Jack?

JACK: We didn't do anything wrong, Babsy.

BARBARA: This can't be right, Jack. I feel like crying.

JACK: I know what you mean.

BARBARA: I'm so sorry, Jack.

JACK: Us Bucks don't feel sorry, Babsy.

BARBARA: At least Martha's all right.

JACK: I bet she is.

BARBARA: You should see her, Jack. A woman sleeping like a baby. Like a baby. I didn't have the heart to wake her up. It's her first good sleep in so long.

JACK: She must be real tired out. Her and her rotten life. How you doing?

BARBARA: I'm okay. Jack, I really do want to go to church. Do you want to come with me?

JACK: No. Thanks. I got to go call the cops. And then somebody ought to be here. In case there's news.

BARBARA: About Lena. Or her baby.

JACK: I'll hold the fort, Babsy. I'll clean up a bit.

BARBARA: I'll make the call, Jack. I'll call the police on my way. There's a phone at the corner.

JACK: Okay, Babsy.

BARBARA: And I'll pray for us both, Jack.

JACK: Good idea, babe.

BARBARA: Oh Jack, look. See in the streetlight? Isn't it lovely?

JACK: Snow.

BARBARA: We'll have a white Christmas after all. I'm going to walk the long way on the way home. Snowflakes, icicles, everything.

JACK:.   Leave it to Joe.

BARBARA: You won't see me till after midnight, till tomorrow. Bye now, see you tomorrow.

JACK: See you tomorrow. Don't get lost now.

BARBARA goes off.

JACK closes the door. He starts to clean the living room, taking notice of the jewellery box, the broken phone, but then stops and just turns the lamp off.

He goes to the closet for his briefcase.

Then he turns on the tape deck for a moment, listens to, say, 'White Christmas.'

Then he turns off the hall lights, turns on those in the up stairwell and heads for the basement door.

He opens it to a green glow.

He stops and looks down, covers his nose and mouth against the reek.

JACK: Holy shit.

He drops his briefcase and freezes.

The up stairwell lights fade.

The snow falls on the porch.

An approaching siren and red flashing lights. All the lights and sound fade.

A shake of jingle bells in the darkness.

THE END

THE AUTHOR THANKS NATIVE EARTH PERFORMING ARTS AND CAHOOTS THEATRE PROJECTS FOR THEIR SUPPORT OF THE DEVELOPMENT AND PRODUCTION OF THIS PLAY. AND FOR THEIR SPIRIT AND FRIENDSHIP, HE THANKS ESPE-CIALLY BEVERLY YHAP AND COLIN TAYLOR.

Daniel David Moses, of Toronto and Kingston, is a Delaware from the Six Nations lands on the Grand River. He lives in Toronto where he writes, and Kingston where he teaches playwrighting as an assistant professor, and Queen's National Scholar at Queen's University. Along with 15 books, Moses has also appeared in *Prism International, ARC, Atlanta Review, The Fiddlehead, Poetry Canada Review, Impulse Magazine, Prairie Fire, QUARRY* and *ELQ/Exile: the Literary Quarterly*, and the collections *Sovereign Erotics: A Collection of Two-Spirit Literature, Native Poetry in Canada, A Contemporary Anthology, Native Writers and Canadian Writing, The Last Blewointment Anthology* and *First People, First Voices*.

Questions for Discussion

1. Discuss the tension between spirituality and materialism and/or the sacred and the profane in one or both plays.

2. Discuss the dramatic function of the character of Clarisse in both plays.

3. Compare the effects of the different dramatic genres and staging conventions used in *Coyote City* and *Big Buck City*.

4. Discuss the relationship between the real and the supernatural in both plays.

5. Discuss Moses' use of the Nez Perce traditional story *Coyote and the Shadow People* in *Coyote City*. Compare it to the Greek traditional story of *Orpheus and Eurydice*.

6. Discuss Moses' reimagining of the Christmas story in *Big Buck City*.

7. Compare the representation of the city in both plays.

8. Discuss the role of Ricky Raccoon as a trickster figure in *Big Buck City*.

9. How and to what effect does Moses make use of stereotypical representations of Indigenous people in both plays?

10. Discuss the use of Indigenous and Christian references and imagery in both plays.

11. Discuss the use of lighting and sound in one or both plays.

Related Reading

Appleford, Rob. Ed. *Aboriginal Drama and Theatre: Critical Perspectives on Canadian Theatre in English*. Vol. 1. Series Ed. Rick Knowles. Toronto: Playwirghts Canada Press, 2005.

Appleford, Rob. "The Desire to Crunch the Bone: Daniel David Moses and the 'True Real Indian.'" *Canadian Theatre Review* 77 (Winter 1993): 12-26.

Brundage, David and Tracey Lindberg Eds. and Daniel David Moses. *Daniel David Moses: Spoken and Written Explorations of His Work*. Toronto: Guernica Editions, 2015.

Episkenew, Jo-Ann. *Taking Back Our Spirits: Indigenous Literature, Public Policy and Healing*. Winnipeg: University of Manitoba Press, 2009.

Gilbert, Helen and Joanne Tompkins. *Post-Colonial Drama: Theory, Practice, Politics*. London: Routledge, 1996.

Moses, Daniel David and Terry Goldie, Preface. "Two Voices." *An Anthology of Canadian Native Literature in English*. Eds. D. Moses and T. Goldie. Toronto: Oxford University Press, 1992.

Moses, Daniel David, "How My Ghosts Got Pale Faces." *Pursued by a Bear: Talks, Monologues and Tales*. Toronto: Exile Editions, 2005.

Nolan, Yvette. Ed. *Performing Indigeneity: New Essays on Canadian Theatre*. Vol. 5. Series Ed. Ric Knowles. Toronto: Playwrights Canada Press, 2016.

THE EXILE CLASSICS SERIES ~ 1 TO 28

THAT SUMMER IN PARIS (No. 1) ~ MORLEY CALLAGHAN
Memoir & Essays 5.5x8.5 280 pages 978-1-55096-688-6 (tpb) $19.95
It was the fabulous summer of 1929 when the literary capital of North America had
moved to the Left Bank of Paris. Ernest Hemingway, F. Scott Fitzgerald, James Joyce, Ford
Madox Ford, Robert McAlmon and Morley Callaghan... amid these tangled relationships, friendships were forged, and lost... A tragic and sad and unforgettable story told in
Callaghan's lucid, compassionate prose. Also included in this new edition are selections
from Callaghan's comments on Hemingway, Joyce and Fitzgerald, beginning in that time
early in his life, and ending with his reflection on returning to Paris at the end of his life.

NIGHTS IN THE UNDERGROUND (No. 2) ~ MARIE-CLAIRE BLAIS
Novel 6x9 190 pages 978-1-55096-015-0 (tpb) $19.95
With this novel, Marie-Claire Blais came to the forefront of feminism in Canada. This is
a classic of lesbian literature that weaves a profound matrix of human isolation, with
transcendence found in the healing power of love.

DEAF TO THE CITY (No. 3) ~ MARIE-CLAIRE BLAIS
Novel 6x9 218 pages 978-1-55096-013-6 (tpb) $19.95
City life, where innocence, death, sexuality, and despair fight for survival. It is a book of
passion and anguish, characteristic of our times, written in a prose of controlled self-
assurance. A true urban classic.

THE GERMAN PRISONER (No. 4) ~ JAMES HANLEY
Novella 6x9 64 pages 978-1-55096-075-4 (tpb) $13.95
In the weariness and exhaustion of WWI trench warfare, men are driven to extremes of
behaviour.

THERE ARE NO ELDERS (No. 5) ~ AUSTIN CLARKE
Stories 6x9 159 pages 978-1-55096-092-1 (tpb) $17.95
Austin Clarke is one of the significant writers of our times. These are compelling stories
of life as it is lived among the displaced in big cities, marked by a singular richness of language true to the streets.

100 LOVE SONNETS (No. 6) ~ PABLO NERUDA

Poetry 5.5x8.5 232 pages 978-1-55096-108-9 (tpb) $24.95

As Gabriel García Márquez stated: "Pablo Neruda is the greatest poet of the twentieth century – in any language." And this is the finest translation available, anywhere!

THE SELECTED GWENDOLYN MACEWEN (No. 7)
GWENDOLYN MACEWEN

Poetry/Fiction/Drama/Art/Archival 6x9 352 pages
978-1-55096-111-9 (tpb) $32.95

"This book represents a signal event in Canadian culture." —*Globe and Mail*
The only edition to chronologically follow the astonishing trajectory of MacEwen's career as a poet, storyteller, translator and dramatist, in a substantial selection from each genre.

THE WOLF (No. 8) ~ MARIE-CLAIRE BLAIS

Novel 6x9 158 pages 978-1-55096-105-8 (tpb) $19.95

A human wolf moves outside the bounds of love and conventional morality as he stalks willing prey in this spellbinding masterpiece and classic of gay literature.

A SEASON IN THE LIFE OF EMMANUEL (No. 9) ~ MARIE-CLAIRE BLAIS

Novel 6x9 175 pages 978-1-55096-118-8 (tpb) $19.95

Widely considered by critics and readers alike to be her masterpiece, this is truly a work of genius comparable to Faulkner, Kafka, or Dostoyevsky. Includes 16 ink drawings by Mary Meigs.

IN THIS CITY (No. 10) ~ AUSTIN CLARKE

Stories 6x9 221 pages 978-1-55096-106-5 (tpb) $21.95

Clarke has caught the sorrowful and sometimes sweet longing for a home in the heart that torments the dislocated in any city. Eight masterful stories showcase the elegance of Clarke's prose and the innate sympathy of his eye.

THE NEW YORKER STORIES (No. 11) ~ MORLEY CALLAGHAN

Stories 6x9 158 pages 978-1-55096-110-2 (tpb) $19.95

Callaghan's great achievement as a young writer is marked by his breaking out with stories such as these in this collection... "If there is a better storyteller in the world, we don't know where he is." —*New York Times*

REFUS GLOBAL (No. 12) ~ THE MONTRÉAL AUTOMATISTS
Manifesto 6x9 142 pages 978-1-55096-107-2 (tpb) $21.95

The single most important social document in Quebec history, and the most important aesthetic statement a group of Canadian artists has ever made. This is basic reading for anyone interested in Canadian history or the arts in Canada.

TROJAN WOMEN (No. 13) ~ GWENDOLYN MACEWEN
Drama 6x9 142 pages 978-1-55096-123-2 (tpb) $19.95

A trio of timeless works featuring the great ancient theatre piece by Euripedes in a new version by MacEwen, and the translations of two long poems by the contemporary Greek poet Yannis Ritsos.

ANNA'S WORLD (No. 14) ~ MARIE-CLAIRE BLAIS
Novel 5.5x8.5 166 pages ISBN: 978-1-55096-130-0 $19.95

An exploration of contemporary life, and the penetrating energy of youth, as Blais looks at teenagers by creating Anna, an introspective, alienated teenager without hope. Anna has experienced what life today has to offer and rejected its premise. There is really no point in going on. We are all going to die, if we are not already dead, is Anna's philosophy.

THE MANUSCRIPTS OF PAULINE ARCHANGE (No. 15)
MARIE-CLAIRE BLAIS
Novel 5.5x8.5 324 pages ISBN: 978-1-55096-131-7 $23.95

For the first time, the three novelettes that constitute the complete text are brought together: the story of Pauline and her world, a world in which people turn to violence or sink into quiet despair, a world as damned as that of Baudelaire or Jean Genet.

A DREAM LIKE MINE (No. 16) ~ M.T. KELLY
Novel 5.5x8.5 174 pages ISBN: 978-1-55096-132-4 $19.95

A Dream Like Mine is a journey into the contemporary issue of radical and violent solutions to stop the destruction of the environment. It is also a journey into the unconscious, and into the nightmare of history, beauty and terror that are the awesome landscape of the Native American spirit world.

THE LOVED AND THE LOST (No. 17) ~ MORLEY CALLAGHAN
Novel 5.5x8.5 302 pages ISBN: 978-1-55096-151-5 (tpb) $21.95

With the story set in Montreal, young Peggy Sanderson has become socially unacceptable because of her association with black musicians in nightclubs. The black men think she must be involved sexually, the black women fear or loathe her, yet her direct, almost spiritual manner is at variance with her reputation.

NOT FOR EVERY EYE (No. 18) ~ GÉRARD BESSETTE
Novel 5.5x8.5 126 pages ISBN: 978-1-55096-149-2 (tpb) $17.95

A novel of great tact and sly humour that deals with ennui in Quebec and the intellectual alienation of a disenchanted hero, and one of the absolute classics of modern revolutionary and comic Quebec literature. Chosen by the Grand Jury·des Lettres of Montreal as one of the ten best novels of post-war contemporary Quebec.

STRANGE FUGITIVE (No. 19) ~ MORLEY CALLAGHAN
Novel 5.5x8.5 242 pages ISBN: 978-1-55096-155-3 (tpb) $19.95

Callaghan's first novel – originally published in New York in 1928 – announced the coming of the urban novel in Canada, and we can now see it as a prototype for the "gangster" novel in America. The story is set in Toronto in the era of the speakeasy and underworld vendettas.

IT'S NEVER OVER (No. 20) ~ MORLEY CALLAGHAN
Novel 5.5x8.5 190 pages ISBN: 978-1-55096-157-7 (tpb) $19.95

1930 was an electrifying time for writing. Callaghan's second novel, completed while he was living in Paris – imbibing and boxing with Joyce and Hemingway (see his memoir, Classics No. 1, *That Summer in Paris*) – has violence at its core; but first and foremost it is a story of love, a love haunted by a hanging. Dostoyevskian in its depiction of the morbid progress of possession moving like a virus, the novel is sustained insight of a very high order.

AFTER EXILE (No. 21) ~ RAYMOND KNISTER
Poetry 5.5x8.5 240 pages ISBN: 978-1-55096-159-1 (tpb) $19.95

This book collects for the first time Knister's poetry. The title *After Exile* is plucked from Knister's long poem written after he returned from Chicago and decided to become the unthinkable: a modernist Canadian writer. Knister, writing in the 20s and

30s, could barely get his poems published in Canada, but magazines like *This Quarter* (Paris), *Poetry* (Chicago*)*, *Voices* (Boston), and *The Dial* (New York City), eagerly printed what he sent, and always asked for more – and all of it is in this book.

THE COMPLETE STORIES OF MORLEY CALLAGHAN (Nos. 22-25)

Four Volumes ~ Stories 5.5 x 8.5 (tpb) (tpb) $19.95
v1 ISBN: 978-1-55096-304-5 352 Pages
v2 ISBN: 978-1-55096-305-2 344 Pages
v3 ISBN: 978-1-55096-306-9 360 Pages
v4 ISBN: 978-1-55096-307-6 360 Pages

The complete short fiction of Morley Callaghan is brought together as he comes into full recognition as one of the singular storytellers of our time. "Attractively produced in four volumes, each introduced by Alistair Macleod, André Alexis, Anne Michaels and Margaret Atwood, and each containing 'Editor's Endnotes.' The project is nothing if not ambitious... and provides for the definitive edition." —*Books in Canada*

And, so that the reader may appreciate this writer's development and the shape of his career – and for those with a scholarly approach to the reading of these collections – each book contains an on-end section providing the year of publication for each story, a Questions section related to each volume's stories, and comprehensive editorial notes. Also included are historical photographs, manuscript pages, and more.

CONTRASTS: IN THE WARD ~ A BOOK OF POETRY AND PAINTINGS (No. 26) ~ LAWREN HARRIS

Poetry/16 Colour Paintings 7x7 168 pages
ISBN: 978-1-55096-308-3 (special edition pb) $24.95

Group of Seven painter Lawren Harris's poetry and paintings take the reader on a unique historical journey that offers a glimpse of our country's past as it was during early urbanization. "This small album of poetry, paintings, and biographical walking tour ought to be on every 'Welcome to Toronto' (and 'Canada') book list. Gregory Betts's smart, illustrative writing, which convinces by style as well as content, and Exile Editions' winning presentation, combine to make *Lawren Harris: In the Ward* a fresh look at the early work of one of Canada's most iconic modernists." —*Open Book Toronto*

WE WASN'T PALS ~ CANADIAN POETRY AND PROSE OF THE FIRST WORLD WAR (No. 27) ~ ED. BRUCE MEYER AND BARRY CALLAGHAN
Poetry/Prose 5.5x8.5 320 pages ISBN: 978-1-55096-315-1 (tpb) $18.95
For decades the literature of Canada's experience in World War One lay ignored and was dismissed by readers, critics, and literary historians. Here, at last, is the imaginative testimony of those who served in the trenches and hospitals of the Great War. These pages chronicle the struggle to put into words the horrors, the insights, and the tribulations that ultimately shaped a nation's character. In the voices of Frank Prewett, W. Redvers Dent, nurse Bertha Carveth, fighter pilot Hartley Munro Thomas, and other members of a generation that gave their lives and their souls to the war, this is the first anthology since 1918 of poetry, fiction, essays, songs, and illustrations that adds an important new chapter to Canada's literature. Preface and Introduction by Bruce Meyer; Foreword by Barry Callaghan; Afterword by Margaret Atwood.

LUKE BALDWIN'S VOW (No. 28) ~ MORLEY CALLAGHAN
Novel 5.5x8.5 196 pages ISBN: 978-1-55096-604-6 (tpb) $19.95
A timeless classic, highly recommended by generations of readers and educators. A story of a boy and his dog and their adventures, which will appeal to the many children – and adults – who are dog lovers. It is also a sensitive story of love and loss, and of making a new life for oneself. Although it was first published seventy years ago, only a few details (such as clothing) really indicate that it is not a contemporary story.

The Exile Classics are available for purchase at: www.ExileEditions.com